MA HOME YOU LOVE

For my parents,
Joan and Paddy McPhillips, without whom ...

First published 2018 by
The O'Brien Press Ltd,
12 Terenure Road East, Rathgar,
Dublin 6, D06 HD27, Ireland.
Tel: +353 1 4923333; Fax: +353 1 4922777
E-mail: books@obrien.ie
Website: www.obrien.ie
The O'Brien Press is a member of Publishing Ireland.

ISBN: 978-1-84717-957-9

Text © copyright Fiona McPhillips, Colm Doyle, Lisa McVeigh
and John Flood 2018

Copyright for typesetting, layout, editing, design
© The O'Brien Press Ltd

Cover design by Tanya M Ross www.elementinc.ie
Design and layout by Tanya M Ross www.elementinc.ie

Edited by Aoife Barrett www.arcadiaps.com

8 7 6 5 4 3 2 1
23 22 21 19 18

Photo credits: Copyright as credited under invididual images. Chapter
opening images: Chapters 1/3/8: Architect DMVF, Photographer Ruth
Maria Murphy; Chapter 2: Architect Plus Architecture, Photographer
Donal Murphy; Chapters 4/5: Architect DMVF, Photographer Paul
Tierney; Chapter 6: Architect DMVF, Photographer Infinity Media;
Chapter 7: Architect Broadstone, Photographer Paul Tierney; Chapter 9:
Architect John Feely, Photographer Ros Kavanagh.

Cover photo credits: front cover: Architect DMVF, Photographer Ruth
Maria Murphy; back cover: Designer Suzie McAdam, Photographer Ruth
Maria Murphy; front flap: (top right) Architect DMVF, Photographer
Ruth Maria Murphy; (bottom left) Photographer Ruth Maria Murphy;
(bottom right) Designer Maven, Photographer Sarah Fyffe; back flap:
(top left) Architect DMVF, Photographer Derek Robinson; (top right)
Designer Dust Design, Photographer Ruth Maria Murphy; (bottom
right) Designer On the Square Emporium, Belfast, Stylist Marlene
Wessels, Photographer Ruth Maria Murphy.

Printed by L&C Printing Group, Poland.
The paper in this book is produced using pulp from managed forests.

Published in
DUBLIN
UNESCO
City of Literature

MAKE THE HOME YOU LOVE

FIONA McPHILLIPS
WITH COLM DOYLE, LISA McVEIGH
& JOHN FLOOD

The Complete Guide to Home Design, Renovation and Extensions in Ireland

THE O'BRIEN PRESS
DUBLIN

Architect: DMVF | Photographer: Ruth Maria Murphy

CONTENTS

Architect: DMVF | Photographer: Ruth Maria Murphy

INTRODUCTION

Make the Home You Love is about utility and it is about beauty, not as an end result but as a process. A home renovation or build is the biggest personal project that most people will ever take on; it requires determination and bravery at every step of the way. The best homes are not the most expensive homes, they are the ones that are the most considered and carefully planned, the ones that reflect the owners' style, personality and commitment. These are the homes that are truly loved.

I started this process, like most people, as a regular punter with limited experience of home design and renovation. By the end of it, like most people, I had a head full of information that had taken years to accumulate and would probably never be needed again. Those coming up behind me asked for advice on architects and planning, taps and tiles. I dutifully passed on my new-found expertise, all the while thinking, there must be a better way. I wrote a piece for the *Huffington Post*, 'How to Survive a Home Renovation', and was blown away by the response. Thus, *Make the Home You Love* was conceived.

I am not an architect, a designer, a decorator. Until a few years ago, I didn't know my lintels from my architraves, my aluclad from my timber. I had never paid much attention to kitchen or bathroom design and I'd certainly never thought about the different types of insulation or roofing. And then I bought a house that was, to put it politely, in need of some modernisation.

A major renovation or build comes with a steep learning curve. Even if you have a professional overseeing the work, it's your money that's being spent and your future quality of life that is at stake, so you need to understand the process, monitor decisions and make choices. By the end of the project, you will care about tiles and toilets, whether you like it or not.

Make the Home You Love is written from the perspective of someone who has been through the entire home renovation process. It will accompany you during the heady days of dreaming about your new home and help you focus on preparation, design and drawings. It will guide you through the stresses of costing and the strains of planning, steer you through tendering and hold your hand during construction when the best paid plans can go awry. Then, when the hard work is done, it will help you put the finishing touches to your interiors and your outdoor space. Of course, a home is never really finished – it will grow and evolve with you and that is part of the beauty of it.

I wish I could say that the book reflects the client I was but that would be untrue. What it does represent is the client I would have been, had I known at the start of the project what I had learned by the end. My wish for this book is to pass on the knowledge and wisdom that Colm, Lisa, John and I have accumulated from both sides of the fence, so that you can begin your journey armed and ready to make the home you love.

Fiona

FIONA McPHILLIPS

Fiona McPhillips is an author, journalist and interiors fanatic. Having survived a complete home renovation and extension, she was inspired to write down all the tips, tricks and techniques she learned along the way, with a little help from the experts. Fiona lives in her never-quite-finished home in Dublin with her husband, three kids, a dog and two cats.

COLM DOYLE BSc.ARCH. B. ARCH (HONS) MRIAI

Colm Doyle graduated in architecture from Dundee University and practised in London with the award-winning Paul Davis & Partners before establishing DMVF Architects in 2005. As an RIAI Grade 3 conservation architect, Colm has a passion for integrating contemporary architecture within historic environments.

LISA McVEIGH BSc. ARCH (HONS) B.ARCH MRIAI

Lisa McVeigh studied architecture at Queen's University, Belfast and worked for Campbell Conroy Hickey Architects in Dublin before setting up DMVF Architects. Lisa specialises in residential projects and has an RIAI accreditation in health and safety and a Grade 3 accreditation in conservation.

JOHN FLOOD DIP. ARCH B.ARCH Sc. (HONS) MRIAI

John Flood studied architecture at DIT, Bolton Street and worked on award-winning projects with de Blacam & Meagher Architects before founding DMVF Architects. John has experience in bar, restaurant and office design, as well as residential projects, and holds an RIAI accreditation in sustainability.

1 PREPARATION

A renovation and extension of the basement in this period townhouse has completely opened it up to the garden.
Architect: John Feely | Photographer: Ros Kavanagh

GETTING STARTED

Most people have some idea of the work and upheaval involved in a home renovation. If you've ever watched 'Grand Designs' or 'Room to Improve' you'll have an insight into the decisions that need to be made, the obstacles you might face and the drama that can unfold on a build, but you never get to see the years of preparation and planning that are involved before any programme begins.

Long before you have chosen a kitchen, before you have ever looked at a floor plan or spoken to an architect, your research will begin. From the first moment you start wishing for a utility room, an extra bedroom or a view of the garden, you will be making plans. In fact, defining what you like about your current home and what you want to change is the first step in the design process.

Whether you are buying a house or an apartment or renovating an existing one, you need to think about your lifestyle and how it fits with where you live now. Do you work from home? Do you spend much time entertaining? Do guests stay over often? Are you planning to have (more) children? How energy efficient is your home? The way you live now and how you plan to live in the future will determine the shape and flow of your home.

It's also important to focus on what you want to achieve as a whole. How do you want your home to make you feel? Do you want it to be brighter, warmer, sunnier? Do you want to make it more modern or more traditional? Do you want a view of a particular tree or breakfast in the morning sun? The experiences your home can give you are just as important as the functional role it plays and the problems it can solve.

Of course, many of these questions may not yet have an answer but that is not a bad thing. The earlier you start your preparation (and you've already begun by buying/borrowing/stealing this book!), the more time you have to look for inspiration and to hone your ideas and your style. Preparation can start months or even years before you ever pick up the phone to a professional. You may even find that what you thought you wanted at the start is very different to what you want after several months of poring over home design books, websites, blogs and magazines. This is the fun part – who doesn't like having a good nose around other people's homes?

The internal walls were removed in this former council house to create an open-plan kitchen, living and dining area.
Architect: Amanda Bone | Photographer: Ros Kavanagh

INSPIRATION IS EVERYWHERE

THE INTERNET

When we bought our house, a 1930s semi-detached in need of complete renovation and extension, friends gave us books and magazines left over from their own revamps. We sat together, admiring photos of minimalist kitchens and extensive glazing, making notes of clever storage solutions and unusual textiles. And then we never looked at them again. It's not that we didn't find them useful or that we didn't appreciate them (thanks guys!), it was just that they only offered a finite selection of what was available and how to achieve it.

With the wealth of design websites, blogs and social networks available online, it is so much easier to find specific inspiration and advice, compare and contrast photos and find your niche, all from the comfort of your own Wi-Fi. Even if you think you know exactly what you want, it's worth spending endless hours browsing design blogs and apps such as Houzz, Pinterest and Instagram to see what other people have done. It will all help

to hone your own style. We certainly found that it helped to crystallise our tastes and find common ground. We had thought originally that we'd decorate the existing house in a traditional 1930s style and have the extension as a contemporary contrast but, thanks to the Internet, we fell so much in love with mid-century furniture that we used some pieces to link the old to the new part of the house.

HOUZZ

Houzz is a home design website and app that also functions as a social network for homeowners and professionals. The main attraction of Houzz is the collection of millions of photos of houses, apartments and gardens that you can save and organise into personal 'Ideabooks'. There is also a large directory of professionals, which you can search by local area, and this is where we found our wonderful architect.

Our mid-century furniture and colour palette helped to link the old and new parts of the house.
Architect: DMVF | Photographer: Ruth Maria Murphy

IT'S WORTH
SPENDING ENDLESS
HOURS BROWSING
DESIGN BLOGS
AND APPS SUCH AS
HOUZZ, PINTEREST
AND INSTAGRAM TO
SEE WHAT OTHER
PEOPLE HAVE DONE.

If you spend enough time on Houzz and save enough photos to your Ideabooks, you will most likely see themes emerging. Maybe all your kitchen photos include bi-fold doors that open onto a patio, or you are drawn to images of integrated, discreet storage. You may also find that your preferences change or that a single photo can inspire you to investigate a new style.

Your Ideabooks and the patterns that emerge from them will help you pinpoint specific ideas as well as an overall look and feel for your renovation and will be invaluable to your architect when the time comes to put it all on paper.

✱ **ARCHITECT'S TIP:** When you save your photos, don't forget to write comments on what you like or dislike, love or hate. This is a great visual way to communicate with your architect.

PINTEREST
Pinterest is a social network that allows users to share or 'pin' photos from anywhere on the Internet onto personalised boards. Boards can have a theme as broad as 'homes' or as narrow as 'polished chrome kitchen taps'. While you can search for something specific, it is also worth viewing the board it is pinned to for inspiration.

Pinterest is useful for all aspects of interior design as you can create boards for single items such as cushions, rugs, paintings and door handles, whereas Houzz tends to focus on entire rooms. Pinterest is also a much more active social network so you might find inspiration from interacting with other people and seeing their ideas.

DESIGN BLOGS
Finding a blogger whose style excites you can give you ongoing motivation for your project. Even if you only connect with one or two, their archives and updates can offer ideas for the

intricate details of your home. Bloggers can also provide a personal context for why certain design decisions were made and give advice on how to create a particular look or mood.

A home design blogger may specialise in a particular style. It could be cool, minimalist Scandinavian homes or dark, rich, tactile interiors or something else entirely, so have a good look around until you find someone who inspires you.

INSTAGRAM
Instagram is a mobile photo and video-sharing social network that allows users to post content on the app as well as on other platforms such as Facebook, Twitter and Tumblr. You can search for any photos that have been posted publicly using hashtags but the best source of inspiration comes from following the accounts of home design magazines, bloggers, interior designers, architects and enthusiasts. Find professionals and amateurs with interesting feeds and check in daily for ideas.

GOOGLE
While Houzz and Pinterest have a seemingly endless supply of home and garden photos, sometimes the quickest and easiest way to find a precise image (e.g. recessed shower shelf) is with a Google image search. This may seem obvious but it's worth mentioning as Google's search algorithms are so much more precise than other tools. The search results will contain not only photos of beautiful, completed shower rooms, but also work-in-progress images and 'how to' DIY advice.

YOUR IDEABOOKS AND THE PATTERNS THAT EMERGE FROM THEM WILL HELP YOU PINPOINT SPECIFIC IDEAS AS WELL AS AN OVERALL LOOK AND FEEL FOR YOUR RENOVATION.

Moodboards will help you identify design themes and patterns for each element of your home and your own style.
Architect: DMVF | Photographer: Ruth Maria Murphy

This north-east facing semi has been opened up to the garden to allow more natural light into the house.
Architect: DMVF | Photographer: Ruth Maria Murphy

OTHER PEOPLE'S HOMES

✱ ARCHITECT'S TIP:
Take photos of everything, as having a file of key images, ideas and products will be invaluable as you move through the project.

While it's easy and exciting to browse photos, there is no substitute for seeing other homes in the flesh. Start looking more closely around friends' houses when you visit and you will notice things that were never on your radar before. Ask questions about which features work well, which don't and what, if anything, your friends would do differently if they were to do it all again. Even if the style isn't one you want to emulate, the functional aspects may be. It's also good to canvass opinions on general issues such as what sort of kitchen layout works best and whether or not a downstairs loo is a valuable addition.

If you live in an area where houses have been built in a similar style, have a look and see what your neighbours have done. Google Maps and Google Earth are good starting points to see the size and scale of extensions, whether they are one-storey or two, how close they've been built to neighbours' houses and how they impact on garden space. You can also look up planning applications on your local authority's website to see the plans that were lodged, if there were objections, what planning permission was granted, what conditions, if any, were attached and whether or not the decision was appealed.

If you see a renovation or extension that you think would work in your house, why not ask the homeowners if you can have a look around? Trust me, people love showing off the fruits of their labour and talking about the minute details of how they achieved it. You spend so much time learning in isolation about insulation, plumbing, flooring, sanitary ware, paint colours, worktops – all information you may never need again – that when someone shows any interest at all, it can open the verbal floodgates. Some people even go so far as to write books about it!

So, don't be afraid to ask for a guided tour. Keep in mind the orientation of the house compared to your own and how the sun travels around the house during the day. Ask the homeowners how the extension is working out for them and if there is anything they would do differently. Look out for things that are specific to the design or location of the house: Are they happy with the size and position of doors and windows? Do they wish they had more light or more storage? Ask them about the planning process: Were there any problems? Did they do anything to avoid potential problems?

✱ ARCHITECT'S TIP: Look out for your local Open House festival. Open House is an annual event in many cities around the world where outstanding architecture is showcased to the public. Buildings that aren't usually accessible open their doors for free and tours are provided by expert guides.

IDENTIFYING YOUR NEEDS

1. WHAT DO YOU WANT TO ACHIEVE?

Whether you want more bedrooms for a growing family, a home office or workshop or a bigger kitchen/dining area for entertaining, you need to think of what you want to achieve from your space. It may be that you have enough physical space already but you need to change it completely to make it work for you. Can a garage become an office? Will a view of the garden make your kitchen a more welcoming place?

Think also in terms of the experiences your home can give you. Do you want to open up the back of the house to bring the outside in? Do you want to look out your bedroom window onto a roof garden? Do you want to see the sky from the bath? This is your opportunity to put them all on your wish list. A renovation is not simply about redecorating or adding a new room.

✱ ARCHITECT'S TIP: Follow the light. Keep an eye on the path of the sun throughout the day. When does it leave and enter the front and rear garden? What is the best way to get more of that daylight into your living spaces?

2. WHAT'S YOUR STYLE?

Once you've collected a range of images, whether online, in magazines and books or in real life, take a step back and look for patterns. Are there recurring colours or colour combinations? Are the rooms minimalist or heavily furnished? Are you drawn to dramatic pops of colour in furniture and fittings? What do you notice about architectural elements like windows, doors, ceiling height and room sizes?

3. ZONE YOUR OPEN-PLAN SPACE

One theme that tends to be in demand across the board these days is the wish for a greater sense of space. Big, open-plan areas with plenty of light are more popular than the traditional design of many small rooms with a similar size and shape. How this open-plan space will be defined needs careful consideration. Do you want a kitchen, dining and living area in the same space? Do you want the sounds of a TV in your kitchen area? Do you need a separate living area? Do you want the kitchen or dining area to open out onto a patio or garden?

While your room should be designed with the different zones in mind, lighting, furniture and finishes can all help to define separate cosy areas in an open-plan space. Think about how you will move through this space and the flow from one zone to another. Make a note of the furniture you want to keep, how this will fit into the space and how you will move around it. Picture the height of the space as well as the floor plans. With an open-plan room, you will have less wall space for pictures, mirrors, shelves and radiators. Underfloor heating eliminates the need for radiators and is a great way of ensuring evenly-distributed heat in a large room.

✱ ARCHITECT'S TIP: An open-plan family room to the rear of the house works really well for everyday functions but is also perfect for family gatherings and entertaining in the evening. Island units are often a great design solution because you can work in the kitchen at the same time as watching the kids or chatting to a friend.

4. BALANCE THE OLD AND THE NEW SPACE

Keep in mind the existing house, how the rooms link together and how they will connect to a new space. If you are adding an extension, will you be restricting natural light in any part of the existing house? Consider using that space for areas that don't need windows, such as utility rooms or cloakrooms.

5. PLAN FOR THE FUTURE

Make sure you think ahead. An open-plan space that works well for young children may not provide the privacy teenagers crave. One family bathroom might be fine for now but what happens when you have several adults fighting for it every morning? If you're hoping this will be the last major renovation you'll ever need, then be sure to consider mobility and access for many years to come.

✱ ARCHITECT'S TIP: In planning for the future, think in chunks of ten years. A deep retrofit and extension of your home will likely last the guts of thirty years. Try and imagine what your family will be like in ten, twenty and thirty years' time.

6. CONSIDER THE NEEDS OF THE HOUSE

While you are clarifying your personal needs, you must also think about the needs of the house. What architectural style is it and when was it built? Where is it located and what is the surrounding landscape like? How does it relate in style and proximity to neighbouring properties? All of these questions are important for planning considerations but should also be at the forefront of any design decisions. The answers will help you to maximise solar gain and views and privacy, while building something new that is sensitive to the original structure.

7. PLAN AROUND YOUR BUDGET

If there's one piece of advice that can be applied to all aspects of home renovation, it's 'Do it once and do it right'. Buy the best you can afford, and that includes professionals. Don't put in a cheap kitchen with a view to changing it in a few years – you will either end up spending too much overall or living indefinitely with a kitchen you don't like.

So how do you buy the best when your budget doesn't seem to allow for it? Economies of scale mean that the most cost-effective way of renovating is to do it all at once. If you can't afford everything you want right now, then plan your renovation in phases that take each other into account. Do the groundwork now. For example, if you want to insulate, then insulate the whole house while you are extending. If you can't afford to decorate at the same time, then do that in phase two.

Don't forget to allow for any professional fees – architect, quantity surveyor, engineer – in your budget. You will also need to hold back a percentage of the total amount for contingencies.

You may also have to factor in the cost of renting during the build. Yes, it's costly, yes, the upheaval is only for a few months, but if you are doing a big job and you value your sanity, you will need to leave the house, if at all possible.

✱ ARCHITECT'S TIP: Trust your architect's advice about build costs. They have likely completed many projects like yours and will be familiar with typical costs for your build type. It is important to be realistic about overall costs from the outset.

ADDING SPACE WITHOUT EXTENDING

Before you embark on a build, consider the space you have and how you can change it. You don't always need to extend to create space – sometimes a clever redesign of existing internal space can deliver what you need at a lower cost.

The first thing you should do is declutter. If you don't use it, get rid of it. Try a car boot sale, a yard sale, donate to a charity shop or recycle – whatever works.

When you've removed all the stuff you don't really need, then take a cleaner, closer look at your home. How much redundant space can you see? Are there rooms you never use? Is there a dark and depressing hallway or corridor? Do you have an unused fireplace and chimney breast taking up space? Think about how these areas could be transformed by changing the internal layout of your home.

Consider vertical as well as horizontal space – raise the ceilings to roof level or install underfloor heating to free up wall space.

You can also reclaim a huge amount of space by using integrated storage – under the stairs, in a kitchen island and recessed into alcoves or walls. Consider buying furniture with storage – footstools, benches and under-bed drawers.

Having a flow of light from room to room can completely overhaul the sense of space in your home. Clear glass panels in doors, walls and even floors can facilitate this but the best way of achieving it is to have a flow from inside to outside. An internal space that opens directly into an outside one makes the internal room feel bigger and makes the garden feel like part of the room.

✳ ARCHITECT'S TIP: Most architects will meet clients in their homes initially so they can get a feel for how the clients use the house, discuss what's not working for them and explore the possibilities available within the budget. This way, it can be possible to solve clients' issues without building an extension.

Making use of all available vertical space provides greater storage options.
Architect: DMVF | Designer: Shalford Interiors | Photographer: Infinity Media

A mezzanine attic level adds a bedroom to this tiny 26 sqm cottage. | Architect: DMVF | Photographer: Ros Kavanagh

ATTIC AND GARAGE CONVERSIONS

An attic or garage conversion can offer a fairly straightforward way of creating a new room as they are generally considered exempt from planning permission. However, there are . still a number of planning restrictions and, as with any building work, you are obliged to comply with the building regulations in your jurisdiction. Ireland has had its fair share of terrible attic and garage conversions, with inadequate head height and staircases, and poorly-planned space, so it's a good idea to get advice from an architect or a structural engineer before you start any work. Remember to check with your local authority to see if your plans are exempt from planning permission.

✳ **ARCHITECT'S TIP:** The floor level of your garage is typically lower than the floor level of your house. If you are in the Republic of Ireland and you choose to raise your floor, check that you will have the minimum required ceiling height of 2.4 metres (m). If you need to raise the roof of your garage, you may need to lodge a planning application.

EXTENSIONS

In the **Republic of Ireland**, you are not likely to need planning permission if the total floor area of your extension is less than 40 square metres (sqm), it's to the rear of the house and maintains at least 25 sqm of garden space. You can use up to 20 sqm of your allowance at first-floor level if your house is detached and up to 12 sqm if it is semi-detached or terraced. There are a number of other restrictions and qualifications so do check with your local authority before you begin any work. The 40 sqm allowance includes all developments so if you are converting or have converted your garage or you have an existing extension built after the introduction of planning legislation in 1963 (whether planning was required or not), then you will have to factor these in.

In **Northern Ireland**, planning permission is generally not required for single-storey rear extensions up to 4 m in depth for a detached house and 3 m for a semi-detached or terraced house, and multi-storey extensions up to 3 m in depth. A side extension should not be more than 4 m in height or wider than half the width of the original house and the floor area covered by the extension and any other buildings (excluding the original house) should not be more than half the total area of the property. Again, any existing extensions need to be included in your calculations. Unless you are building a conservatory, the materials used in exterior work should be similar in appearance to those used in the existing house.

There are a number of further restrictions in both jurisdictions. For example, in the **Republic of Ireland**, Velux windows to the rear of the house are usually exempt, whereas those on the side or front elevation need planning permission. In **Northern Ireland**, they do not need planning permission but are subject to certain restrictions. So please check with your local authority to see if your plans fall within the limits of permitted development.

Legislation and regulations are subject to change and the information here is included only as a general guide. It's important to confirm with your local authority and/or a suitably-qualified professional that the proposed works are compliant with all relevant legislation and regulations within your jurisdiction. The best thing you can do is to get this in writing before starting work on any build.

ARCHITECTS

DO YOU NEED AN ARCHITECT?

This is probably the question I am asked most so I will give you a clear and precise answer: Yes.

If you're doing any sort of structural design work then yes, you need an architect. Yes, even if your brother-in-law's cousin is an engineer/quantity surveyor/brickie and has built an extension with her bare hands. In fact, especially if your brother-in-law's cousin is an engineer/quantity surveyor/brickie and has built an extension with her bare hands.

Your architect will navigate the entire project, from design to planning, from tendering to snagging. They will make the best use of your space and will find design solutions to problems you didn't even know you had. Your architect is the person you will rely on throughout the project for advice and moral support, and is the one who will basically talk you down from the ledge when you're standing in a pile of rubble, looking at a hole in the roof that you're pretty sure was not in the plans.

Many people imagine that an architect simply draws up plans and then their work is done – that's what I thought. Knowing a few architects, I realised that they trained for at least seven years but I never really thought about what they learned in the same amount

Extensive glazing and a patio fireplace encourage outdoor living in this garden room.
Architect: DMVF | Photographer: Ros Kavanagh

This extension to a 1950s cottage added a new kitchen, living and dining space, along with a workshop and artist's studio.
Architect: ALW | Photographer: Ros Kavanagh

of time it takes to become a doctor. It turns out they know all about design, engineering, building, materials, planning, regulations, tendering, compliance, project management and most importantly, people management. And they've been through the entire process many times before.

If your budget allows, then you should get yourself a good architect to manage the whole project and you will cut your workload by 90 per cent. But what about the cost? Fees are negotiated on an individual basis depending on the location, scale, complexity and site conditions, and can often add up. However, the cost of inexperience can be so much more. It can lead to design mistakes and administration errors, and poor personnel management can mean delays that result in a far greater overspend. Also, your architect will have a relationship with tradespeople and suppliers, which may be of benefit to you.

The other way in which your architect will prove their worth is by undertaking regular site visits to monitor and inspect the work, and to keep on top of your builder's progress. This is the sort of clout and background that no individual client will have, regardless of how confident they are about managing the build.

If you just can't justify the additional cost or if you are just making some small changes to your home then it is still worth asking an architect to come and look at your home and advise you on your options. Some will make an initial visit free of charge but it can also be valuable to pay for some advice to get you started. Another option is to book a consultation through the charity-driven RIAI Simon Open Door initiative or the Royal Society of Ulster Architects (RSUA) and PLACE Ask an Architect week (see *Resources*). For a relatively small donation, you will get an hour with an architect.

If you decide to make any structural changes to your home then do get an architect to draw up plans, even if they are not going to oversee the build. All the renovations I've seen that don't quite work share one feature – they were not designed by architects. Use your budget wisely and don't skimp on professional advice in favour of furniture or fittings that can be added at a later stage.

So how do you find a good architect? A personal recommendation is always best – ask your family, friends, colleagues and online acquaintances. Look at the recommended architect's website for photos or visit the finished product, if possible, to get a feel for the style and quality of their work. The RIAI website has a directory of registered architects in the Republic of Ireland, as does the RSUA website for Northern Ireland. Houzz also has a large directory of professionals with photos of their work.

If you find an architect whose work you like, call and organise a visit to your home to get a feel for their design ideas and to see if they match with your own. Remember, you will be working closely with this person for many months so make sure you are comfortable with everything. Once you've found someone you like, ask for references so you can talk to people they've worked with. The key phrase is 'made it all so easy' – if you get that feedback, you're onto a winner.

APPOINTING AN ARCHITECT

Once you've chosen your architect and agreed on the scope of the work, a contract is drawn up. There are a range of sample contracts suitable for all types of builds in the **Republic of Ireland** on the RIAI website. For projects in **Northern Ireland**, you can purchase contracts from the Royal Institute of British Architects' bookshop.

An architect's fee depends on the requirements and scale of each project. It can be calculated as a percentage of the total construction costs, agreed as a lump sum or charged at an hourly or daily rate, although the most commonly used option is the first one. The fee is usually paid in stages that coincide with the standard work stages of the project.

✳ ARCHITECT'S TIP:
Ensure your architect is a registered member of the Royal Institute of Architects of Ireland or the Royal Society of Ulster Architects by checking their online directories.

This staircase was built in an internal courtyard between the original nineteenth-century house and a new extension.
Architect: DMVF | Photographer: Paul Tierney

WHAT DOES YOUR ARCHITECT DO?

INITIAL DESIGN
At this stage, you will prepare a brief while a survey of your site is completed. Your architect will prepare a proposal and work with you to come up with an overall layout and design for your project.

DEVELOPED DESIGN
At the second stage, you and your architect will develop the design and all associated considerations, including your planning application. This stage is necessary whether or not planning permission is required.

DETAIL DESIGN
This stage involves finalising all the details for building, electrical, plumbing and engineering work and consulting with the relevant professionals and bodies to develop and action tender documents.

CONSTRUCTION
The final stage includes inspection of the build, overseeing the payment schedule to your builders, snagging and certification. In some ways, this is the most important time to have an architect on your side as problems arise and timelines extend.

DO YOU NEED A QUANTITY SURVEYOR (QS)?

A quantity surveyor is a building professional who has expert knowledge on construction costs and contracts. Whether or not you should use one depends on the scale and complexity of your project. Generally, you can never have enough advice. If the project is relatively small and straightforward, your architect should be able to guide you through the cost analysis. However, if you are working with a protected structure or a building that might have significant hidden unknowns, then a QS will be of huge benefit. Similarly, if your project is extensive, you should consider using a QS, who is likely to save you money in the long run. For example, having a QS prepare a cost plan in advance will help avoid any major cost overruns once your build has begun.

YOUR BRIEF

Once you've considered all aspects of what you want your project to achieve, you can begin preparing your brief. The list of twenty questions here is a great starting point and the answers will contain much of the information that your architect or builder will need to know.

The visual mood boards you have prepared online and the photos you have gathered from books and magazines will be of the utmost importance to your architect – even if you can't define your style, they will see a pattern in your images.

Next, you should go through your home room by room and make a list of all the features and amenities that you would like to have. Of course, not all of these will carry the same weight – some may be essential whereas others may be simply a distant dream. One way to prioritise is to divide the features into a 'must-have' list and a 'wish' list. Another option is to rate each item from one to four, depending on how important they are to you. Try to keep your budget in mind when preparing your brief but do allow yourself to dream just a little bit – there are often ways and means of achieving your heart's desire!

20 KEY QUESTIONS TO ASK YOURSELF BEFORE YOU START

1. What do you like about your current home?

2. What do you dislike about your current home?

3. Do you want to extend or change the space you have? Or both? Why?

4. If you are extending, what function(s) do you want the new space to have?

5. Are you prepared to go through the planning process?

6. Describe your lifestyle. Do you spend a lot of time at home? Do you entertain often? Do guests stay over often? Are you planning to have (more) children?

7. How much time do you spend in each of the rooms of your home?

8. What new spaces do you need?

9. What style of architecture and interior design do you like?

10. What style is the existing house? Do you want to change this?

11. What style do you want the extension to be?

12. Is sustainable development and increased energy efficiency important to you?

13. How long do you intend to stay in your finished home?

14. Have you future-proofed your plans?

15. Do you need to consider mobility or age-related issues (for yourself or anyone else who might be staying in the house)?

16. Will you be living in the house while the work is being done?

17. What is your budget?

18. When would you like to start and/or finish work?

19. Who will be the primary contact for the professionals involved in your project?

20. How involved (or not) do you want to be in the project?

Architect: DMVF | Photographer: Ros Kavanagh

When the going gets tough, just picture yourelf relaxing in your beautiful new home. | Designer: Maven | Photographer: Sarah Fyffe

NEIGHBOURS

Don't forget to think about your neighbours and the effect an extension will have on them. Will it reduce their light or cause overshadowing? Will they have an overbearing view of the wall of your extension? Talk to them and try to involve them in the process. Talk to others in the area about how extensions have affected them, any problems they've had and any steps they've taken to overcome them. Look at planning permission that has been awarded on your street to see examples of what is allowable and what residents can live with – if it has been done several times already, then it is probably reasonable.

On the other hand, don't give in too much to others' demands. Sometimes people's initial reaction to change is to be wary of it. Hopefully, once you have sat down and talked through the plans, a solution can be reached. If not, ask your architect to meet with your neighbours to try to find a solution everyone can live with.

You should also talk to your neighbours about the noise and disruption that will happen when the build starts so they are prepared for what's to come and have a chance to voice any concerns.

LOOKING AFTER YOURSELF

It's going to be fun, it's going to be exciting but you can be certain it's also going to be stressful at times. When the going gets tough, you need to be able to do two things – to take a step back and look at the bigger picture and to keep an eye on the prize. In other words, your home will still be beautiful, even if something goes wrong, and it will be finished eventually, even if that sometimes seems like a long way off. In the meantime, you need to look after yourself and, if you are renovating with a partner, you need to make sure you don't kill each other. Be prepared for your relationship to be tested and plan to take time out from the build so you can talk about something else for a while. Go away for a long weekend and let your architect worry about the dry rot in the attic.

A renovation takes courage and ambition. You need to be able to embrace change and upheaval and you need to have faith in your ideas and your team, even when you're standing in that pile of rubble, looking at that hole in the roof. In fact, that's when you need it the most. You will survive, your home will be beautiful and it will be all because of you.

1950s DETACHED HOUSE

WHO LIVES HERE:
Sarah Clarke, her husband
and three children

LOCATION:
Rathfarnham, Dublin 14

PROJECT:
Complete renovation
and extension

A U-shaped extension using natural stone makes the most of the morning
and the evening light. All images in case study:
Architect: DMVF | Photographer: Ruth Maria Murphy

Rear view of original house.

THE PROPERTY

When Sarah and her husband bought their
arts and crafts house in Rathfarnham, it
needed a huge amount of modernisation.

After five years of living in it, they knew
exactly what they wanted to do.
**'I wanted to drag it into the twenty-first century,'
says Sarah. 'It needed good insulation, good
windows and a good flow. Basically, I wanted
good family living in a comfortable home.'**

Sarah had a fairly clear idea of the style she
wanted to achieve.
**'I kind of know what I like – a mix of antiques,
mid-century and modern furniture. I'm not
drawn to sterile modern looks but I do like really
clean lines and a mix of materials that gives a
warm aesthetic.'**

THE PREPARATION

Sarah took to the Internet to prepare her brief for her architect, who had been recommended by a friend.

'I looked at Houzz and Pinterest to develop a sense of what was out there and collected images for each space, and I consulted with my friend Tom, who has a background in interior design.'

One specific photo caught Sarah's attention, although it wasn't one she had planned to replicate.

'The image that ultimately resulted in the curve on our staircase was one I'd saved from a loft apartment in the States. I just saved it because I liked it, not because I thought we could integrate something like it.'

However, Sarah's architect showed the photo to a metalworker and he was able to recreate the style on her staircase.

'It was a collaborative process between myself, Tom, my architect and the metalwork guy. It was a process that evolved from a collection of images that were then teased out and made to work for our space.'

Now the image of the curve on Sarah's staircase is an inspiration for others.

'I look at the photo of our staircase now and think, oh my God, that's gorgeous. And it was almost a happy accident.'

Original living room.

Original kitchen.

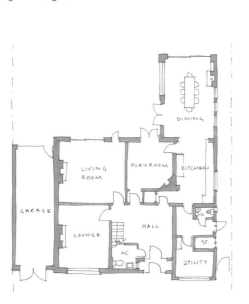

Original house plan.

New house plan.

THE BEST BITS

The living room sofa, with its view of the garden, is one of Sarah's favourite places, although she admits she has several spots that she loves.

'The three garden-facing rooms capture the light differently throughout the day, which is really great.'

She also appreciates the flow through the house, which works perfectly for them.

'I just love that it's a great family space.'

+ 'I LOOK AT THE PHOTO OF OUR STAIRCASE NOW AND THINK, OH MY GOD, THAT'S GORGEOUS. AND IT WAS ALMOST A HAPPY ACCIDENT.'

2 DESIGN

✳ ARCHITECT'S TIP:

Inevitably, the design will evolve and change along the way. Remember that the design process includes everything from foundations and drainage to electrical and plumbing layouts. It is important that you are flexible throughout the design process as you may have to make changes to solve problems that come up.

＋ MAKE EVERY CHOICE PART OF THE OVERALL DESIGN PLAN.

Photographer: Ruth Maria Murphy | Interior Designer: Suzie McAdam

WHAT IS DESIGN?

'DESIGN IS A PLAN FOR ARRANGING
ELEMENTS IN SUCH A WAY AS BEST TO
ACCOMPLISH A PARTICULAR PURPOSE.'
– *CHARLES EAMES*

Design is all about making things work. Good
design offers an intuitive solution to a problem.
Great design marries form and function,
bringing joy to the user in the process. A good
example is Harry Beck's London Underground
map. Originally printed in 1931, and the
blueprint for all future designs, it has become
an instantly-recognisable London icon.

A common mistake is to view design as
something done at the end of a project to tidy
it up, instead of seeing it as the entire process.
Even the visual part of design is not solely about
decoration – every aesthetic cue should have its
own function within the overall plan. For example,
colour and lighting can set a mood or evoke an
emotion and materials can serve a tactile or visual
purpose as well as a functional one. Whether you
are choosing a kitchen or a lamp, try and think,
what am I trying to achieve in this room? Rather
than simply choosing a lamp because you like
the look of it, think about what sort of lighting
it will bring to your room, where you will put
it, how you will access it and how it will fit with
its surroundings. Make each choice part of the
overall design plan.

Of course, you may not know exactly what you
want or need. Design is an evolutionary process
that adapts to change and is as much about
finding problems as it is about solving them.
Good communication is the key to doing this. The
more detailed and personal your brief, the more
your designer will understand your objectives,
even if you can't yet see them clearly yourself.

HOLISTIC APPROACH

It's important to look at any project in terms of
the wider environment it inhabits, particularly

for architectural design. This holistic approach
takes into consideration people, context,
orientation, sustainability and neighbouring
properties, along with the building itself. While
all aspects of home design are interconnected,
I've divided them into three core elements – the
people around whom the home is developed,
the place in which the building resides and the
space within it.

This house, built on an old, sloped potato field, has been
inspired by the physical characteristics of the landscape.
Architect: McNally Morris | Photographers: Alan Bennett,
Dominic Morris

PEOPLE

This is all about you. Your home is your own
personal space and should be designed around
the relationships, lifestyle and traditions that
will develop while you live there. This design
will have a huge influence on your daily lives,
how you interact with each other and how
you experience the passage of time across the
seasons and the years.

When you are writing your brief, think about how you live now but also how you expect your lives to change over time. Include children (at every stage), elderly relatives, pets, work, mobility or age-related issues, and anything else that might need consideration. A full renovation should last for several decades so try and think in blocks of ten years. If your children are young, imagine them as teenagers and again as adults. If you plan to retire in the next ten or twenty years, picture yourself at home full-time and imagine how you might use your home then.

Once you have mapped out future transitions, you can start looking at the present. What do you want from your home? What do you need? What do you love and hate about your current home? What styles of architecture and interior design do you like? What is your budget? The list of '20 key questions to ask yourself before you start' in *Preparation* is a great beginning point. The answers to these questions should be part of the first brief you send your architect, builder or designer.

First and foremost, your home should be functional and that means it should be built around the needs of you and your family. That doesn't mean it can't also be beautiful, but if it doesn't facilitate your lifestyle then it hasn't been designed properly. Make sure your brief includes a list of 'must-haves' first and a 'wish list' second. For example, if plenty of storage and a spare room are essential then put them on the first list. If you'd love a kitchen island but not at the expense of a utility room, then prioritise accordingly.

Even storage can be beautiful as well as functional.
Architect: DMVF | Designer: Shalford Interiors | Photographer: Infinity Media

YOUR NEIGHBOURS

Don't forget the neighbours – neighbours are people too! And they're going to have to look at the outside of your home for a long time to come. Listen to their concerns and try to balance them with your own plans. A renovation can strain the best of relationships so it is a good idea to try and come to an amicable agreement before you start. But don't be pressured into making changes you're not happy with, especially if your architect feels that your plans are reasonable and, if planning permission is needed, that you are likely to succeed in getting it.

AFTER YOUR PROJECT IS
FINISHED, YOUR HOME
SHOULD FEEL LIKE IT STILL
'FITS' IN ITS LOCATION.

The materials and design of this forest retreat take their cues from the surrounding landscape.
Architect + Photographer: Alan Bennett Architects

PLACE

Place or context refers to the location of a building and it encompasses all the external elements that can influence design and development. These can be physical, such as trees, landscape, roads and nearby buildings, or non-physical, such as culture, climate and cost. All of these aspects can have a significant influence on the design process in terms of architectural style, size and materials. With residential development, place or context also includes clear planning rules and guidelines.

After your project is finished, your home should feel like it still 'fits' in its location.

That's not to say that it should be identical to other properties in the area, nor should it simply blend into the surrounding landscape. However, the design does need to take its cues from its environment and any renovation or extension should respond to the original building. This response can also be complementary, for example where a contemporary extension on an older house uses traditional materials. This sense of place gives your home an identity and a perception that it belongs to the community, a quality that in turn transfers to you, the owner.

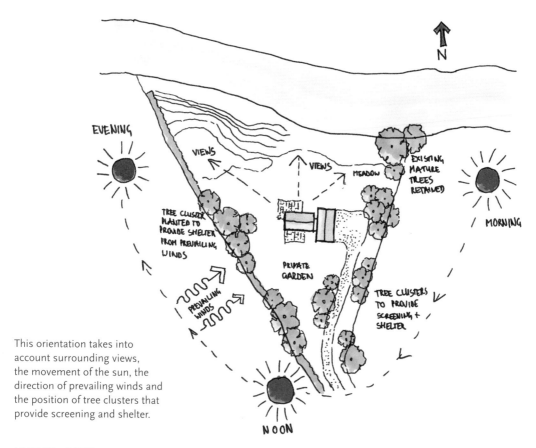

EVENING

MORNING

NOON

N

VIEWS

VIEWS

MEADOW

EXISTING MATURE TREES RETAINED

TREE CLUSTER PLANTED TO PROVIDE SHELTER FROM PREVAILING WINDS

PREVAILING WINDS

PRIVATE GARDEN

TREE CLUSTERS TO PROVIDE SCREENING + SHELTER

This orientation takes into account surrounding views, the movement of the sun, the direction of prevailing winds and the position of tree clusters that provide screening and shelter.

YOUR SITE

The specific area on which the building rests is called the site. Your site may be several acres or it can be 10 square metres (sqm) at the back of your house. This is your canvas and the starting point for your design. Important site considerations include landscape, orientation, access, privacy and adjacent buildings.

In design terms, orientation describes how a building is positioned in relation to the movement of sunlight during the day and throughout the year. A good orientation ensures that your home will maximise sunlight when and where it is needed, while also preventing glare and overheating during the warmer months. It is also concerned with wind patterns. You'll often hear orientation referred to in terms of the direction in which your home or garden points, e.g. a south-facing garden.

How light enters and moves through a room and how shadow is cast across a garden should be one of your greatest design concerns. Plot the movement of light across your site from

sunrise to sunset and from summer to winter. Sun position calculators are useful visual tools for this (see *Resources*). Knowing how much light you have in a room at a particular point in the day will help you to lay out the interior of your home. For example, a sunlit living or eating area may be something you prefer to have in the morning, whereas others may prioritise it for evening time. It will also allow you to visualise the effect the position of new doors, windows and roof lights will have on your home.

Orientation is also important in maximising solar gain – the amount of heat from the sun that is retained in the house. Solar gain is one of the principles of passive design, a method of construction that uses windows, walls and floors to collect, store and distribute solar energy. A passive heating system reduces or eliminates the need for auxiliary heating or cooling. You can find out more about passive design for homes at the Passive House Association of Ireland (PHAI) and the

Sustainable Energy Authority of Ireland (see *Resources*).

If you are extending or renovating an existing house, you may think orientation is out of your hands. However, the shape of your extension and the position of glazing is still a prime concern. For example, the back of our house faces north-east so it gets the sun in the morning, while the front is flooded with light in the afternoon and evening. So, in order to take advantage of as much light and heat as possible, we designed an L-shaped extension to the rear, which captures the sun as it moves around the side of the house. This, along with a large rooflight, ensures that the back of the house is warm and bright all day long.

Your architect will carry out a full site analysis before any drawings are developed. This is a record of all the data related to the site and its context and includes orientation, aspect, topography (the shape and features of the ground on and around the site), existing buildings and materials, existing landscape features, boundary treatments and the prevailing wind direction.

> ✳ **ARCHITECT'S TIP:** With rising energy prices, improving energy efficiency has become a key issue. It is important to consider how you can remodel your home for better orientation to benefit from the natural sunlight that will fill your home and from the free warmth that the sun provides.

This house has been redesigned with extensive glazing and insulation in order to take advantage of solar gain.
Architect: DMVF | Photographer: Paul Tierney

Rear view of original house.

SPACE

The space you design should fulfil your needs at all times of the day and night, during each season of the year and for decades to come. Make sure your space works as hard as you need it to. Picture yourself undertaking various daily tasks at different times in each space. For example, a daytime work space can become a living or eating area in the evening, while a playroom might develop into an office or guest room in time. Imagine each space on a bright summer's day and on a cold, wet winter's evening. If you plan carefully, you can ensure that each room functions well, regardless of external influences.

From the start, you should consider furniture layouts and storage requirements as they will affect the shape and the flow of the room, as well as the functionality. With clever storage and optimal use of your space, you may not need as large an extension as you think or you may not need one at all.

Once you have decided how many bedrooms and bathrooms are possible and what you want from your kitchen and living areas, you can start thinking about the shape and form of your space and how you want it to make you feel.

Light, colour and texture all interact to contribute to the visual impact of a room and the emotions it triggers. Each element has such a strong influence on the other that they should be incorporated together into your design plan rather than chosen individually. Begin by asking yourself what mood you want to inspire in each room – you might want a living room to be relaxing, a kitchen to be stimulating and a bedroom to be luxurious. Your lighting design, colour scheme and materials can facilitate this and should be considered from the start, along with the room shape, size and layout.

Design alone won't determine exactly how you will behave in a space but by taking into account general and cultural responses and looking at what inspires you personally, you can create a home that will enhance your mood and increase your sense of wellbeing.

THE SPACE YOU INHABIT SHOULD SERVE A FUNCTIONAL PURPOSE BUT IT SHOULD ALSO PAY ATTENTION TO YOUR SOCIAL AND PSYCHOLOGICAL NEEDS.

The bookcase peninsula divides the two spaces in this open-plan room.
Architect: DMVF | Photographer: Laura O'Gorman

The soft colours and textures work together to make this a relaxing room.
Architect: DMVF | Photographer: Paul Tierney

In contrast, the hard materials and darker colours in this room concentrate the focus on eating and entertaining.
Interior Designer: On The Square Emporium, Belfast | Stylist: Marlene Wessels | Photographer: Ruth Maria Murphy

LIGHT

Light allows us to put a shape on the world around us. It's not just the quantity and source of light that matters but also the contrasts it offers, the interplay of light and shadow in a room and how this shading moves over time. These changes affect our perception of colour, texture and space to the extent that the same room can have a different atmosphere depending on the time of day or year.

Daylight stimulates growth and activity in all living organisms and it has a physiological impact on people, maintaining our biological rhythms and hormonal cycles. Studies have found that daylit environments increase workers' productivity and sense of comfort, and a connection with the outdoors provides the mental and visual stimulation to promote health, healing and learning.

While orientation and glazing influence the amount of natural light entering a home, how people perceive each room also depends on the characteristics of the surfaces within it. Light changes as it is absorbed and reflected so the materials and colours you choose, and where you position them, have a significant effect on the mood created. For example, gloss cupboards reflect light and can make a kitchen seem bigger but can also feel cold and harsh if they are combined with a reflective tiled or concrete floor. In contrast, a wooden floor can bring a softer edge to a room while rugs, cushions and curtains can add colour, texture and warmth. Even the fabrics you choose affect the behaviour of light – satin and silk reflect it, velvet absorbs it and rough-textured fabric casts shadows upon itself.

TYPES OF LIGHTING

There are three basic types of lighting that you should consider:

1. Ambient lighting – provides even, overhead light to a room, usually in the form of a ceiling pendant or recessed lights. Wall-mounted sconces can also achieve this. It's preferable to have ambient light on a dimmer so you can control it, depending on your mood or the time of day.

2. Task lighting – helps you perform specific tasks, such as reading, cooking or eating. Table and floor lamps provide task lighting in the living room and the bedroom, while under-cabinet lighting and pendant lighting work well in the kitchen. Bars and sconces are most commonly used in bathrooms, providing light around mirrors.

3. Accent lighting – brings drama and visual interest to a space by highlighting features such as art, plants and bookcases. Table lamps, wall-mounted picture lights and strip lighting along shelves all create focal points in a room.

This house was opened up to the outdoors to take advantage of the beautiful garden, which was designed by Diarmuid Gavin. | Architect: DMVF | Photographer: Ros Kavanagh

A SPACE THAT IS FULL OF DIFFERENT TYPES OF LIGHT AND SHADE IS RICH WITH VISUAL FORCES THAT DRAW THE EYE AND STIMULATE OUR EMOTIONS.

In the initial design stages, think about where you will place furniture and appliances, how each part of a room will be lit during the day and at night, and how light will flow from one space to the next. Put your utility room, storage and bathrooms in areas without much natural light and turn alcoves and corners into reading nooks using lighting and soft furnishings. With a considered lighting design plan, you can make use of every inch of your space.

Another type of lighting that can have a great visual impact is garden lighting. If you are using large amounts of glazing or glass screens, then having light outside when it is dark turns glass from black to transparent and creates a connection between the house and the garden. Accent lighting that highlights specific plants and trees can look stunning from inside.

In the image below, the recessed ceiling light provides ambient lighting for the whole room. There is task lighting either side of the mirror and accent lighting highlights the shelves.

1. Task lighting can also help create a reading nook or corner.
Designer: Maven | Photographer: Sarah Fyffe
2. This bathroom uses all three types of lighting. | Architect: DMVF | Designer: Veronica Clarke | Photographer: Paul Tierney

LIGHTING DOS & DON'TS

- **Do** consider furniture layouts before deciding on lighting.

- **Do** provide task lighting for work surfaces, such as kitchen counters and dining tables.

- **Do** provide reading lights at seating areas and bedsides.

- **Do** aim for pools of light and shade as this will make a cosier atmosphere.

- **Do** use both dimmer and regular switches.

- **Do** use a mix of hidden/recessed and feature lighting.

- **Do** ensure all bulbs give a warm glow rather than a cold white light.

- **Do** provide good lighting at mirrors in bathrooms.

- **Do** consider garden lighting.

- **Don't** rely solely on ambient lighting.

- **Don't** have too many lighting circuits.

- **Don't** pepper the ceiling with recessed downlights.

- **Don't** forget to include a switch for bedroom lights at the bed-head.

- **Don't** forget to have a light in the attic and in other storage locations such as the hot-press and cloakroom.

✱ ARCHITECT'S TIP: If your renovation budget doesn't stretch to garden lighting, ask your electrician to provide the cable and switching anyway. This is the cheaper part of the process and light fittings can be added at a later date.

COLOUR

Colour is one of the properties of light so the two should be considered together. When light hits a surface, some of it is absorbed and some of it is reflected – the light that is reflected contains the colour that we see. As the quality and quantity of available light changes, so too does our perception of the colour of an object. At varying times of the day and the year, a room can look very different; natural and artificial light can also create very separate moods. When we look at an object or a space, usually the first thing we notice is its colour and its shape, then we recognise its texture. Form and finish quickly pass from memory but colour remains and informs our recollection. So, while we may not remember the pattern of a wallpaper, we will remember that it was blue and our impression of that blue is largely dependent on how the light and shadow fell on it when we saw it.

Not only do we remember colours, they can also invoke an emotional response by triggering our mental reactions. Colours can agitate or relax, stimulate or soothe. When you are creating your space, it is crucial that you take into consideration how you want the room to make you feel. While soft greens and greys generally promote feelings of tranquillity and yellow is associated with vibrancy, how each colour impacts on you can also depend on your style, your age and your culture. The best way to explore colour without making a commitment is to create some moodboards on Houzz, Pinterest and Instagram. You can also virtually paint a drawing or photo of your room using Photoshop or an online tool or app – many paint manufacturers have these on their websites.

Think also about the flow of colour from room to room and how each space looks and feels when the doors are open. For example, a glimpse of luxurious navy or purple can offer

INTERIOR DESIGN IS PART OF THE BONES OF THE BUILDING, WHEREAS INTERIOR DECORATION IS WHAT HAPPENS ON THE SURFACE, THE FINAL LAYER.

a cosy invitation to a living room, while a cool grey hallway provides the necessary calm when you return from a long day's work.

TEXTURE

Texture is the tactile quality of the surface of an object, whether it is rough or smooth, hard or soft, matt or gloss. While the physical nature of texture lends itself to a specific functionality, for example, stone to floors and worktops or wool to armchairs and rugs, it also has a strong visual presence that can transform a room. How the texture of one object is perceived depends largely on its interaction with light and the colours and other textures surrounding it. Light-reflective materials, such as metals, polished stone and gloss finishes, bounce light around the room, and colours on these surfaces tend to look brighter and stronger. Textures that absorb light, such as matt paint, wool and velvet, have colours that appear darker and subtler.

Contrasting textures create balance in a room. Without contrast, the eye is drawn to nothing in particular and the most beautiful surfaces can become overlooked. Texture is particularly important if you are working with a limited or monochromatic colour scheme, as it will bring depth and divergence to your room.

While you don't have to worry too much about textiles and soft furnishings in the initial design stages, you should give plenty of thought to any new flooring, kitchen finishes, windows, doors or colour schemes you want to include and how they will work with your existing furniture and fittings.

This velvet sofa absorbs the light, giving it a dark and subtle colour.
Designer: Maven | Photographer: Sarah Fyffe

INTERIOR DESIGN

Interior design is something that begins on day one of the design process and evolves and adapts as you move through each stage of the project. It deals with form and function, creating an interior environment that fulfils your needs, represents your style and enhances your quality of life. It is often confused with interior decorating, which is concerned with creating a style or a mood by embellishing and enhancing existing surfaces. In other words, interior design is part of the bones of the building, whereas interior decoration is what happens on the surface, the final layer. But you know that by now!

While you don't have to start picking out bed linen and blinds right away (but if you are like me, feel free to obsess), most design elements that involve plumbing or electrics need to be agreed before you can look for a builder. That means you have to decide on the placement of sanitary ware in your bathroom, and appliances and sinks in your kitchen and utility room, the layout of entertainment and media systems, and your lighting design. You will need to consider the location of furniture in relation to your TV, audio equipment and lighting, and think about the flow and passageways around your furniture, especially in an open-plan room with several zones.

✱ **ARCHITECT'S TIP:** Don't take yourself or your interiors too seriously! Try to add humour to your spaces. Colours, pieces of art or textiles that encourage a smile are always a welcome addition.

Top: This sheepskin rug provides balance with the stone floor.
Interior Designer: Dust Design | Photographer: Ruth Maria Murphy
Bottom: The intensity of a darker wall here is broken up by a large feature mirror, which bounces light around the room.
Interior Designer: Kingston Lafferty Design | Photographer: Ruth Maria Murphy

It can be tricky to get electrical layouts right, particularly in bedrooms. Take some time to consider the position of beds, wardrobes and desks or you may end up with sockets behind large pieces of furniture or on the opposite side of the room to a desk. We managed to get this wrong in all three children's bedrooms due to deeper than average wardrobes and an unforeseen purchase of a loft bed. So now they have to deal with annoying cables and awkward sockets until they can afford to move out. (Sorry – at least our own bedroom is fully functional!)

While you're considering room layouts, you will no doubt also be thinking about the style of furniture and fittings, colours and textiles. This is all discussed in more detail in the *Interiors* chapter, so feel free to take a sneak peek as interior finishes and decoration is something that will most likely be on your mind throughout the project. Keep checking Houzz, Pinterest and interiors blogs as well for ongoing inspiration and trend updates.

ELECTRICAL LAYOUT DRAWING

An electrical layout drawing shows all the light fittings and switches, appliances, heating and controls, and sockets.

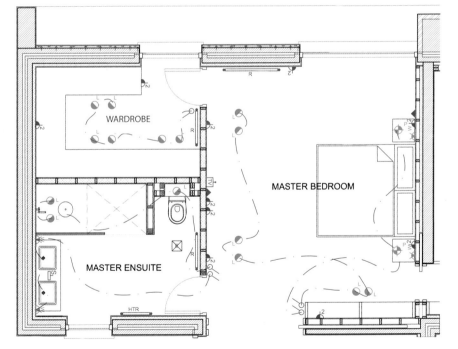

1970s DORMER BUNGALOW

WHO LIVES HERE:
Naomi Morley, her husband and two children

LOCATION:
Bray, County Wicklow

PROJECT:
Renovation and extension

This 1970s bungalow was transformed into a contemporary family home.
All images in case study: Architect: DMVF | Photographer: Paul Tierney

Front view of original house.

THE PROPERTY

In 2015, while they still were living in Australia, Naomi and her husband bought a dormer bungalow near Bray Head, County Wicklow.

'My husband is from Bray and I'm from Dalkey so we know the area,' says Naomi. 'We got it at a great price so we totally took a punt on it.'

Without having seen the house, their initial brief was very basic and, although they knew they wanted a contemporary design, they didn't have a clear idea of how this would develop. They sent the brief to three architects and did a Skype call with each one to decide which one would suit them best.

THE DESIGN

The architect they chose impressed them with his research and his consideration of all the factors affecting the design.

'In the drawings, he showed us the orientation of the house and how the sun travelled around the house and this was something we had never even considered.'

As Naomi and her family would be in Australia for the entire design process, they needed someone they could trust to listen to them and develop the contemporary look they wanted.

'He took into account all our requirements without trying to push us one way or another and we knew early on that he was on the same wavelength regarding design.'

The design process took three months of Skype calls and emails, and thirteen sketch schemes until they felt it was exactly right.

'I found the design process very interesting and we found the whole project a really great experience. I felt our architect really cared about it and that's so important in the design phase.'

Original kitchen.

Original dormer bedroom.

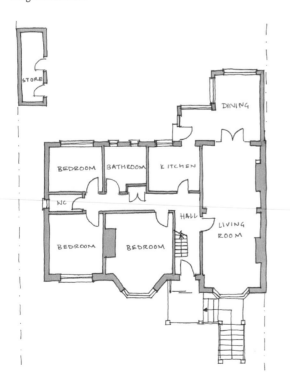

Original house plan.

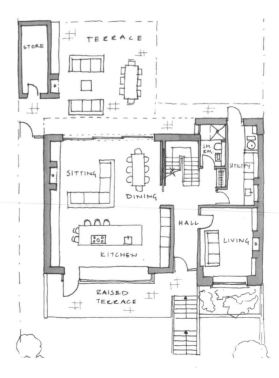

New house plan.

THE BEST BITS

Having lived in Australia, Naomi was used to the idea of a connection between the outside and the inside space, and she wanted to recreate this in her new home in Bray.

'That open-plan room becomes so big once the sliding doors are open. When you're in the back garden, you can see through the whole house all the way to the view at the front. I love the whole feeling that the outside is part of the house.'

Open-plan living was a big, positive change for the family.

'I don't even mind cooking now,' says Naomi. 'The kids can play in the garden and I can be peeling vegetables and watching them at the same time.'

Naomi also loves the storage in her home. 'We have places to put everything. The bench in the open-plan room has drawers that pull out and all the kids' toys get thrown in there. It's a really easy house to manage.'

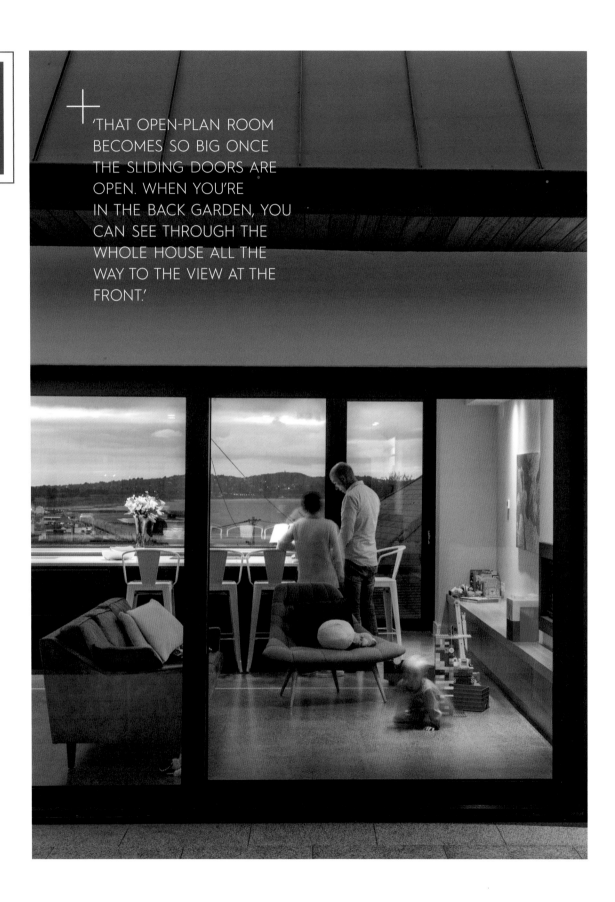

'THAT OPEN-PLAN ROOM BECOMES SO BIG ONCE THE SLIDING DOORS ARE OPEN. WHEN YOU'RE IN THE BACK GARDEN, YOU CAN SEE THROUGH THE WHOLE HOUSE ALL THE WAY TO THE VIEW AT THE FRONT.'

3 DRAWINGS

Our challenge was to take a neglected 1930s house and coax it into the twenty-first century, while holding on to everything that made it wonderful in the first place.

GETTING STARTED

Architectural drawings are the technical plans that describe the design of a building. They are developed over a period of time, in an organic process that is as much about problem solving as it is about creating a finished product. Along the way, many potential solutions are put into context to see which features work best. Could a must-have cloakroom fit under the stairs or should you take some space from another room? Can you work out a way to increase the amount of light in your hall? Do you really need a kitchen island if a peninsula gives you more storage space?

Most people have never looked at an architectural drawing before they are presented with their own set. Don't feel intimidated if at first you find it hard to make sense of it all. It doesn't take long to become familiar with the layout, especially in the context of your own home.

Once you have discussed your brief with your architect, they will work with you to come up with an initial design. It's very rare that a first sketch will become the end product. Be prepared for many meetings with your architect, where you draw and redraw certain elements of the design. These drawings will become more complicated as you move through the design stages. Don't be tempted to rush through this first stage. Be sure you are happy with everything as it is laid out and don't be afraid that you are 'causing trouble' or putting your architect out by asking for changes. It is so important to get your drawings exactly right before you enter the planning and tendering phases, as any changes you need to make after that are likely to cause delays and incur costs.

✱ **ARCHITECT'S TIP:** Although relatively standardised, every architect has their own drawing style. If you don't understand something in the plans or the terminology used, don't be afraid to say so. You won't be the first person to ask what a section is or what the word elevation means.

All images in this chapter: Architect: DMVF | Photographer: Ruth Maria Murphy

THE DESIGN PROCESS

The architectural design process begins when you present your brief to your architect. Your key questions, your lists of options for each room and your photographic moodboards will all help to describe your style and your vision for your home. Then, following a site analysis, your architect can advise on construction costs and begin working on an overall design for the project. This schematic design is a clearly-defined concept for the proposed structure of your home and your architect may develop a number of sketch schemes to try and test out different design approaches.

When you have decided on an overall design, you can work out the finer details of each area in your design plan during the stage known as developed design. This is where you'll nail down specific dimensions and work on heating, plumbing, electrical, audio visual and built-in and custom items. If you need planning permission, your architect will work on planning drawings at this stage.

Once all your design decisions have been made and any necessary planning permission has been granted, you will move on to the detail design stage where your architect will prepare the construction drawings. These are much more detailed drawings that communicate all necessary information to building officials, builders, materials suppliers, engineers and other professionals. Every aspect of how a project is to be put together must be included in these drawings. Construction drawings are discussed in more detail in the *Tendering* chapter.

TYPES OF DRAWINGS

- The first drawing your architect will give you is a floor plan, which is a flattened, 2D view of a floor level from above. This is the drawing that will tell you the most about a building, from the type and the size, to the shape and layout of rooms, the location of doors and windows and much more. Your architect may begin with a hand drawing while you flesh out ideas together. Then you should receive computer-generated plans of your existing home and the proposed changes or simply the plans for your new build if you are starting from scratch. All measurements will be in millimetres (mm) so teach yourself to think in lengths of 1000 mm if you are more used to metres (or yards if you are old school).

While floor plans will give you precise dimensions for each room and the features they contain, it is often difficult to visualise the finished product from just one perspective. Often, other drawings are also needed:

- An elevation drawing is a 2D representation that shows the upright part of a building, usually the front, back or the side. It is the view you see when standing on the ground and looking at a wall. An internal elevation drawing is a depiction of an internal wall. It is often used to show kitchen design, carpentry or a fireplace.

- A section (or cross-section) drawing represents a vertical cut through a room or a building so that you are looking towards an internal wall. These are often the drawings that people find hardest to visualise. A section through a room can be likened to an apple that has been sliced in half lengthwise, the core and pips clearly visible. It differs from an internal elevation drawing in that you are looking at all parts of the room from the point at which the cut is made, not simply a single wall or upright feature.

- You may also get 3D drawings but keep in mind that these don't usually come as standard so make sure to ask your architect in advance whether or not they are included in the fee. A 3D drawing can be a great help if you are finding it hard to imagine your finished home using 2D plans alone.

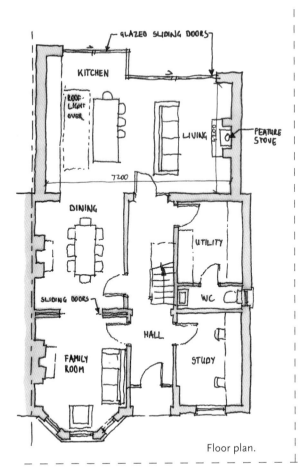

Floor plan.

Elevation.

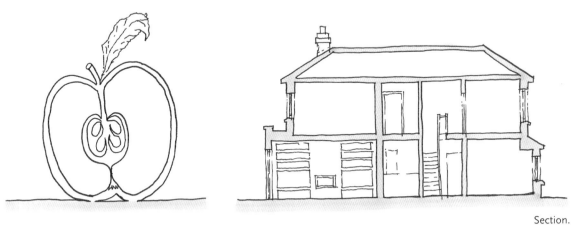

Section.

A SECTION THROUGH A ROOM CAN BE
LIKENED TO AN APPLE THAT HAS BEEN SLICED
IN HALF LENGTHWISE, THE CORE AND PIPS
CLEARLY VISIBLE.

3D drawings can help visualise 2D plans.

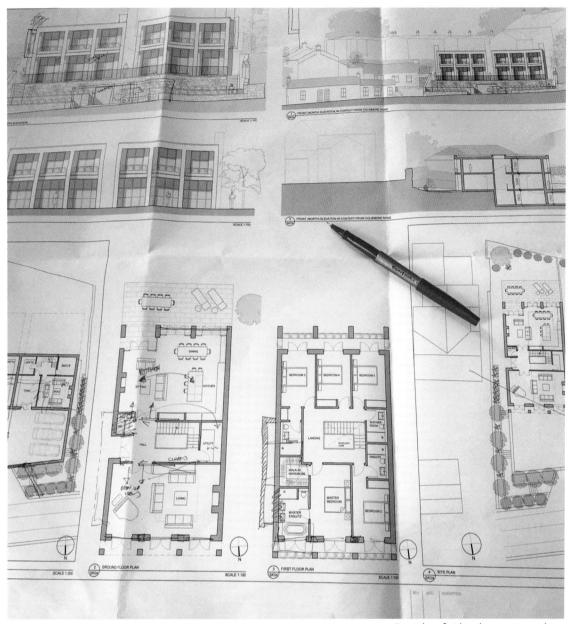

Don't be afraid to draw on your plans.

Architectural or sketch drawings can sometimes appear to be quite formal but when you receive them, don't be afraid to write on them, draw on them, copy them and do whatever it takes for you to feel comfortable with them. There's plenty more paper in the printer and it's important for you to be as familiar as possible with your plans.

✻ **ARCHITECT'S TIP:** Drawings are not simply technical plans to be used for planning and construction purposes. From the earliest stages, you should consider furniture layouts. From sketch design onwards, you should be considering how many kitchen units you can have and how much wardrobe space you can fit in each of the bedrooms. All of these items should be reflected in the drawings.

OUR STORY

Instead of showing you random floor plans and elevations and trying to explain the elements of each, I'm going to take you through the development of my own house design, from brief to final drawings. The process took longer than expected and pushed our budget higher than planned but, now that we are on the other side, I am thankful for every delay, difficulty and disappointment. The problems meant we (literally) had to go back to the drawing board and find a better solution. As I said before, do it once and do it right.

In 2013, my husband and I bought a 'blank canvas' property, in other words, a shell. It was a double-fronted, semi-detached house with a garage and a large rear garden. Apart from the addition of a couple of electrical sockets, the house had not been updated since it had been built in 1934. It needed rewiring, replumbing, central heating, insulation, new windows, new floors and a kitchen. I don't mean a new kitchen, I mean it didn't have a kitchen. All it had was an original scullery with sink and stove which was still (barely) functional.

On the plus side, the house did have all its original features and, because it had never been built on or altered in any way, most of those features (archways, doors, architraves, picture rails, fireplaces) were in relatively good nick. It was kind of adorable; it just wasn't liveable.

Our 'blank canvas' purchase.

ORIGINAL FLOOR PLANS OF OUR HOUSE

The original house was 124 square metres with front and rear living rooms, a scullery and a garage downstairs, and four bedrooms, a bathroom and a separate toilet upstairs. The floor plans display the position and layout of each room. The plans show the relative thickness of walls and openings to represent doors and windows. Each door is drawn in its open position, while the windows are indicated by three parallel lines. The chimney breasts and fireplaces are shown protruding from the walls. There is a side passage to the right of the house and the left side is connected to the house next door (No. 21).

As there was no built-in cabinetry anywhere in the house, it is easy to look at the floor plans and picture the shape of each room and to see how they relate to each other. The best way to do this is to walk yourself through the house and try to visualise the features of each room as you enter it.

The front living room has a three-sided, Victorian-style bay window that is represented by three openings at the front of the floor plan. Opposite are partition doors separating the two living rooms – these are shown recessed into the walls on either side. There are fireplaces in both living rooms, the bedrooms above them and one in the scullery behind the garage. Upstairs, the four bedrooms, bathroom and toilet open off a central landing.

Our house faces south-west to the front and north-east to the back. This means that we get sun in the morning at the back of the house and all afternoon at the front. The bottom half of the garden also catches the afternoon and evening sun.

Original house plan – downstairs.

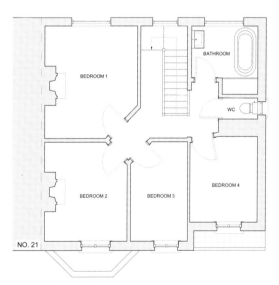

Original house plan – upstairs.

Original front living room.

Original kitchen.

Rear of the original house.

ELEVATION DRAWINGS

The elevation drawings give you a better idea of the style of the house. This is what you see standing on the ground outside the house and looking at the three external walls. The shape of the front, rear and side is more apparent in this drawing, as is the aesthetic view of the windows, doors and brickwork on the bay window in the front living room.

SECTION DRAWING

This section or cross-section view of the house shows a cut through the living rooms and the bedrooms above them. The front of the house is to the left and the rear is to the right. If you imagine that the house has been sliced from top to bottom through the bedrooms upstairs and the living rooms downstairs and you are standing facing the walls with the fireplaces in all four rooms, it is easier to visualise this. Behind you is the rest of each room, the hall and landing and the other side of the house. This view is simply a section through these rooms, to help us see the vertical detail in each room. It also shows the wall, floor, ceiling and roof heights, shapes and thicknesses.

Elevation drawings of the original house.

Section drawing of the original house.

OUR BRIEF

When we bought the house, we had three children, aged nine, five and three, a large dog and two cats. Each family member had their own requirements and some of the tribe were getting bigger and more demanding all the time. In a decade, we'd have three teenagers; in two, we'd be on our own again.

We knew from the start that we wanted to add a large kitchen/living/dining room at the rear of the house – a communal area that was completely missing from the original house. With an almost 30m long garden, there was plenty of scope to extend and still maintain a space big enough for all of us to enjoy outdoor living. In our brief to our architect we said:

'We spend a lot of time in the kitchen so we want that to be a living space, a comfortable environment where we can cook, entertain, relax, watch TV, read and the kids can do their homework. We also plan to make good use of the garden so we want the kitchen to open onto the garden so that the outdoor space is an extension of the kitchen area. We have three kids, a dog and two cats so there will be plenty of movement from kitchen to garden.'

This communal area was really the crux of the whole design and half our wish list was taken up with features for this new room, including a wood-burning stove, a kitchen island, space for a tall fridge and freezer and an eight-seater dining table. Keeping the front living room relatively unchanged would mean that we'd still have a separate space for the inevitable times that one of us wanted to get away from the others.

Although there were already four bedrooms, two of them were very small so we hoped to build a fifth, which would be the master bedroom. We also wanted to convert the garage to an office as I work from home (spoiler alert: I am writing this in said converted garage).

What was less clear to us was what we should do with the rest of the downstairs space. An extension would block the flow of light into the back living room and into the hall, which was already quite dark and gloomy. We also needed to accommodate a utility room and a bathroom. On his first visit, our architect saw the solution. He suggested we take out the chimney breast in the scullery and the separate toilet upstairs and move the stairs into that space, giving a clear run through the hall to the extension; double doors with glass panels leading into the extension would allow light to flow in both directions for the entire length of the house. You're hired!

The original hall was dark and gloomy.

INITIAL DESIGN

The other major issues were teased out during the initial or schematic design stage. Our architect presented us with four different sketch schemes and, after discussing the pros and cons of each, we decided to split the rear living room into a utility room and a cloakroom/storeroom. These are both rooms that do not require natural light, as ambient lighting is usually fine for the tasks that need to be carried out there (ironing, sorting clothes, searching frantically through drawers for a tool that isn't where it's supposed to be). As the back of the house faces north-east, we decided on an L-shaped extension that would catch the sun as it moved around the side of the house. However, because of this sun pattern, we would need to build the new bedroom on the right-hand side so as to avoid excessive overshadowing of our neighbour's property to the left. We knew from the start that we would need planning permission so our architect kept planning issues in mind throughout.

DEVELOPED DESIGN

Once we moved into the design development stage, we focused on room layouts, the position of doors and windows, sanitary ware, kitchen units, storage, shelving and materials, while our architect consulted with an engineer on structural issues. At this stage, you will carry a measuring tape in your pocket at all times and will spend a truly astounding amount of time looking for furniture and fittings of a precise width.

This is the time for you to think in terms of how whole rooms will fit together, when there is still a chance to tweak your drawing dimensions if necessary. For example, if you've always wanted a super king size bed then make sure that your door and window openings are positioned appropriately, and that you have allocated the necessary space for bedside tables and wardrobes. Or if you plan on having a stove, think about how you will position your furniture, TV and shelving or storage in relation to it, and also where you will keep your logs or other fuel. You should also start making decisions about sanitary ware, tiles and flooring, all of which may have long lead times between ordering and delivery.

Make copies of your floor plans, enlarge them, draw on them and cut them up. Cut out shapes of your furniture to the same scale and move them around the floor plan to get an idea of where they fit best. Measure the space around them on the floor plan and use the scale to get a feel for how your arrangement would work in real life. Are you comfortable walking past a sofa that is only 500 mm from the coffee table? Is there a better configuration for your furniture or do you need to rethink the shape of the room? Never trust your eyes to make these judgements – keep that measuring tape in your pocket and it won't let you down.

✱ **ARCHITECT'S TIP:** When preparing the drawings for your home, don't forget storage. From an early stage on all projects, it is important to include space for the vacuum cleaner, mop and bucket, ironing board, sweeping brushes, tool kit, laundry baskets, coats, school and sports bags, shoes, filing, clothes horse/rack and so on. These items will all need to be accessed regularly but storage for them often isn't considered until people move in – when you might need to build another extension to accommodate them!

DEVELOPED DRAWINGS FOR OUR HOUSE

The finished drawings show the changes in the internal structure of our house, as well as the details of our extension.

ORIGINAL HOUSE AND FINAL DESIGN: GROUND FLOOR

BEFORE   **AFTER**

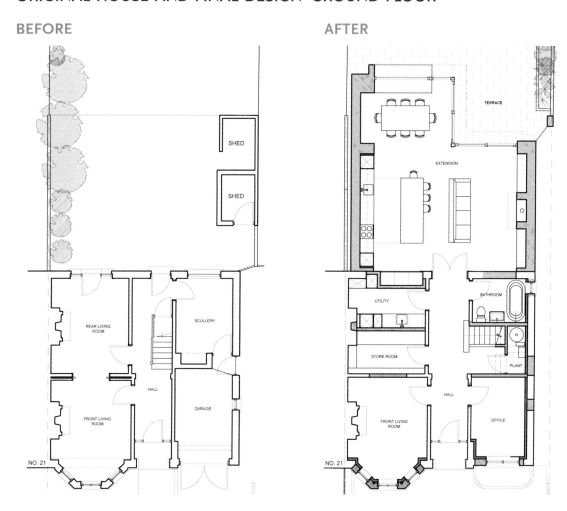

ORIGINAL PLANS

The finished floor plan shows the extensive changes we made to the ground floor. The front door now leads to a bright and airy hall with six internal doors leading off it. At the end of the hall, glass-panelled double doors lead into the extension. As you enter the house, the office is on the right and now has a window to the front instead of a garage door. The partition doors in the front living room have been taken out and the wall has been closed up to create a snug, self-contained space.

Moving down the hallway, the new stairs are to the right, under them is a little playroom and behind them is a plant room. You may be wondering why we would have a tiny, windowless room for displaying our plants – I know I was! Turns out this is architect-speak for the boiler room.

Opposite is the storeroom and at the end of the hall, we have the bathroom to the right and the utility room to the left.

If you look closely at the utility room wall on the floor plan, you can see that there are three kitchen units recessed into the other side of the wall. These units are actually in the kitchen and the utility wall is built around them, allowing them to be flush with the main kitchen wall – a nice example of a clever storage solution.

Walking through the double doors into the extension, the recessed units are directly to the left with the rest of the kitchen units running along the left-hand wall. A kitchen island with seating is in front of this and there is a separate dining area behind it.

To the right is a living area with a fireplace, incorporating a new chimney breast, and recessed shelving either side, and there is glazing all across the back of the room.

1. The new front living room
2. The playroom under the new stairs.
3. The dining area of the extension.
4. The kitchen.
5. The downstairs bathroom.
6. The internal window seat is matched by an external one.
7. The living area of the extension.

ORIGINAL HOUSE AND FINAL DESIGN: FIRST FLOOR

Upstairs, we reclaimed some floor space in the area of the old staircase, while the new one sits in the space formerly inhabited by the chimney breast and toilet. The existing bedrooms are largely unchanged, while the bathroom has been re-configured in the new floor space and the window has been moved. There is also a new rooflight over the bathroom, shown by the broken line next to the window, and another over the stairs.

The big change to the upstairs layout is the addition of a master bedroom behind the bathroom. On the right, the new chimney breast protrudes from the wall but this is hidden behind wardrobes. To the left of the bedroom, you can see a large rooflight over the kitchen below.

MAKE COPIES OF YOUR FLOOR PLANS, ENLARGE THEM, DRAW ON THEM AND CUT THEM UP. CUT OUT SHAPES OF YOUR FURNITURE TO THE SAME SCALE AND MOVE THEM AROUND THE FLOOR PLAN TO GET AN IDEA OF WHERE THEY FIT BEST.

AFTER

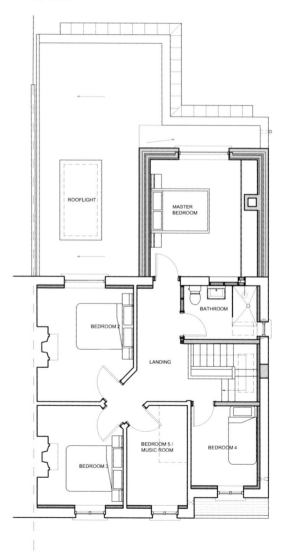

BEFORE

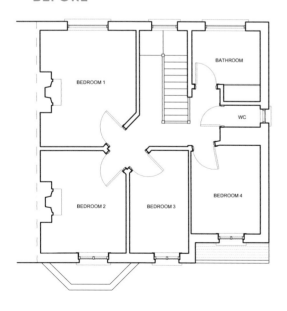

1. A wet room style shower and screen gives a greater sense of space. 2. The addition of a roof light means the stairwell is flooded with natural light. 3. The dark walls give a richness and sense of luxury to the room. 4. I'm very proud of my DIY Ikea hack wardrobes and homemade linen lampshade.

FINAL DESIGN: ELEVATION DRAWINGS

This elevation drawing shows the new rear of the house with the ground floor extension and the new master bedroom on top of it. You can see that the roof of the dining area slopes upwards (a mono-pitch roof), something that is not apparent from looking at the floor plans alone. However, as this is a 2D drawing, it is difficult to see the L-shape of the new ground floor room and you can't see any of the details on the side of the dining area or the side wall of the new bedroom and living area.

Detail that is missing from the rear elevation can be seen in the side elevation drawing. Here you can see the shape of the external window seat, the sliding doors into the dining area and a clerestory window above them – this captures the sun as it moves around the house. The new windows and roof lights in the existing house are also visible.

New rear elevation drawing.

The extension.

New side elevation.

FINAL DESIGN: SECTION DRAWINGS

For the vertical detail inside the house, you need to look at section drawings. This is the same view of the house as the 'before' section drawing earlier in the chapter. If you are standing at the front of the house, the cut goes through the bedroom and the front living room to the left of the front door and continues all the way through the house to the new dining area. As you face this section of the house, the new living area and bedroom above are behind you. What you can see is the new layout of the existing house, with the rear living room now split into a cloakroom and a utility room, and the full length of the new kitchen and dining areas. The layout of the kitchen units and the raised roof light above them is detailed, as well as the internal and external window seats.

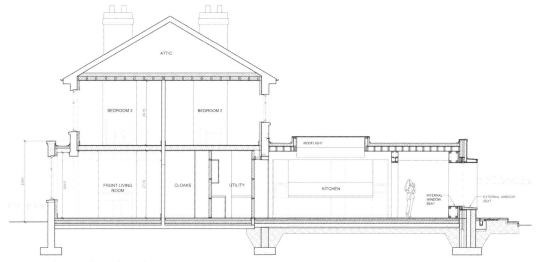

New section drawing from the side.

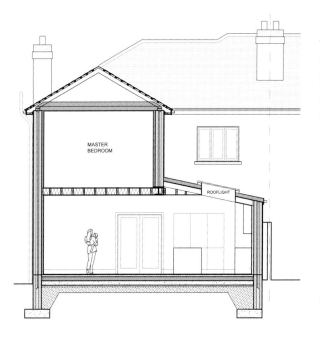

This section is a view through the extension. Imagine you are standing in the back garden looking at the rear of the house. The cut removes the back wall of the house so you can see right through into the rooms.

New section drawing from the rear.

FINAL DESIGN: 3D DRAWINGS

Sometimes, even with the amount of detail found on floor plans, elevations and sections, it can still be difficult to visualise a certain part of a home design without seeing it in its full 3D glory. When we were designing the mono-pitch roof over the kitchen and dining areas in the extension, we needed to get a better feel for how it would look from the outside and from above. The 3D drawings allowed us to visualise this perfectly, giving us a more realistic impression of the finished product. They are also a great way to try out different materials and finishes.

New 3D view from the rear.

New 3D view from above.

WHY I LOVE MY HOME

Did I mention yet that I love my home? Every morning, I get up, walk down the stairs and I can't believe my luck. A large part of that joy comes from the work that went into it, not only the renovation itself but also the eight years of saving and searching before we found it. I love that every part of it has its own story, from the vintage furniture finds to the DIY Ikea hacks, from the under-stairs playroom to the art-filled bathroom.

While the planning and the research sparked our excitement, it was the drawings that brought our dreams to life and gave us a common focus. They made us realise not only the significance of the design as a whole but also how important it was to focus on every detail, however small.

As the house was in such a derelict state when we bought it, every single aspect of it had to be considered. So now, whether I'm looking at our floor tiles or worktops, shutters or taps, I remember the hours of Internet research, the quest to find the most affordable options, while keeping the vision alive. Where there's a will, there's a way, especially when it comes to interior design. But that's for another chapter.

There's not one single thing that I love most about our house. I adore the Victorian hall floor tiles that I worked so hard to fit into our budget. I'm proud of the photo wallpaper at the top of the stairs, and the G Plan chairs that are the result of a hardcore Internet search. But most of all, I love the openness at the back of the house – the light, the space, the view. There is nothing like curling up on the window seat with a book and a full view of the garden, connected to, yet insulated from, the world outside. It's such a peaceful place that often, nobody even notices you're there. Apart from the cats, who live there. Such clever creatures.

While the mood of each room varies, we carried the colour palette of blue/grey/green with pops of yellow and orange throughout the house.

4 COSTS

The natural stone finish on this extension continues into the garden on the patio and raised beds.
Architect: DMVF | Photographer: Ruth Maria Murphy

COSTS AND COMPROMISE

Let's get one thing straight from the start – this project is going to cost more than you think. If your only experience of home renovation comes from TV shows, then you could be in for a nasty shock. Renovation shows often get big discounts from the professionals and suppliers they feature and they can give the impression that the house has been fully fitted out and furnished at a cost way below market prices. Even if you have researched every aspect of your project meticulously and you are lucky enough not to have any big surprises along the way, there will be something that adds to the cost. It could be that it takes an extra week to get your electricity connected while you twiddle your thumbs in your overpriced rental, or the culprit might be that beautiful parquet flooring you saw on Houzz last week that you just can't stop thinking about.

So be prepared for compromises on your costs and be ready to adapt. No matter how carefully you budget and how strictly you stick to it, you will never know the final cost until the project is finished. And keep in mind that sometimes a problem can present an opportunity. When we discovered that our floor joists were rotten and we would have to pour concrete, we used the opportunity to put in underfloor heating as it was only a small increase on the cost of the concrete floor. Now I don't know how we ever survived without it.

DO IT ONCE AND DO IT RIGHT

When (I mean if, of course!) you discover that your budget is not equal to your ambitions, you will need to make some tough decisions. The best way to do this is to think about your long-term goals. For example, if you are certain you will need an extra bedroom or an en suite at some stage down the line, then take steps to ensure that these goals will be met, if not now, then at some point in the future.

1. PRIORITISE STRUCTURAL WORK

If your budget won't cover everything in your plans, make sure to focus on any necessary structural work. Non-structural work, such as decorating, furnishing and landscaping, should be the first thing bumped from the list. You have the rest of your lives to put the finishing touches to your home but any structural work that you put off is likely to cause huge upheaval and cost considerably more at a later date than if you get it done now. Even if you are only doing a small amount of renovation work, this principle still applies. If you are decorating room by room but you also want to insulate, do all the insulating, plastering and electrical work in one go and leave the painting and decorating until you can afford the time or money to get it done.

2. THINK LONG TERM

While you might be tempted to cut expensive yet invisible items such as insulation or a new boiler, you need to think ahead to the potential ongoing costs of decisions like these. If, for example, your heating bills are going to increase by more (over a five- to ten-year period) than you are saving, then it is a false economy.

You can also plan your work in phases if your budget does not currently stretch far enough. If you know there will be a phase two at some point in the future then you can prepare the infrastructure now. For example, if you can't afford that second storey right now, put in the necessary foundations so you can do it at a later stage. You have the builders and tradespeople on site so make the most of them – plumb for the utility room you haven't fitted out yet or put in cabling for the solar panels you'll get next year.

3. BUY THE BEST YOU CAN AFFORD

Don't be tempted to use cheap finishes, planning to change them in a year or two. If you do this, it is not simply the cost of the kitchen or sanitary ware that needs to be considered, you also need to factor in labour, skips, new fittings, the possibility of having to move pipes and electrical sockets and of course, the hassle of it all. And if you never get around to changing it, you'll have lingering pangs of remorse hanging around your beautiful new home. Spend a little extra now and you will save money in the long run.

4. TAKE YOUR TIME ON INTERIOR DESIGN

Furniture should be the very last thing you include in your budget. It is something you shouldn't rush into buying anyway. Until you have a clear understanding of the interior design plan for each room, don't be tempted to buy a sofa or a coffee table in isolation just because they are on sale. Once you've got a bed to sleep in and a chair to sit on, you'll survive while you save for the furnishings that will bring you joy every day. Your home does not have to be perfect before you move into it – don't forget, many of us spent our childhood years watching TV on hard kitchen chairs while our parents saved up for a three piece suite.

FACTORS AFFECTING COST

1. SIZE

Size is the biggest determinant of cost. Building or renovating simple, square buildings is cheaper than creating ones with many angles or curves but, in general, the bigger the area, the greater the cost. Having said that, what's going on inside your building will also have a big impact – complex layouts and details will take longer and cost more.

2. LEVEL OF FINISH

The level of finish can vary hugely and it's at fit-out stage that you tend to see budgets going bust. For example, a kitchen can cost a few thousand euro or tens of thousands. Each decision you make, from flooring to paving and tiles to taps, impacts your budget and just a few hundred extra here and there can push you over the edge. The good news is that plenty of research and shopping around can pay off, with sales and discounts often available locally or online. And allowing yourself to splurge on one or two luxury items can give a high-quality feel to an otherwise low-cost finish. For example, you could buy a plain porcelain toilet and hand basin and spend your money on taps – they are the only thing people will notice. Choose your favourite luxury paint colour and find a similar colour in a cheaper brand. Keep an eye on second hand websites for fixtures and furniture – if you know exactly what you need, you can set up an email alert for a specific search term. I spent months waiting for a response on my search terms 'mid-century', 'sideboard', '150cm' in the price bracket €0–150, but that horse came in eventually and I snapped it up within minutes of getting an alert.

3. PROJECT MANAGEMENT

Hiring a professional (architect/quantity surveyor/engineer/project manager) to manage your project will add a significant chunk to the cost but do keep in mind that the price of not hiring one can be higher. Any mistakes in the build or simply a lack of proper coordination

1. A natural stone worktop is hard-wearing and long-lasting but can make a significant dent in your kitchen budget. | Architect: DMVF | Designer: Newcastle Design | Photographer: Mark Scott

2. Natural materials such as linen, stone and solid wood create calm, light-filled interior spaces. | Interior Architecture: Maria Fenlon | Photographer: Sean & Yvette

3. Solid timber kitchen doors will cost you more than vinyl or foil-wrapped but are easier to paint, if you fancy a change. Architect: DMVF | Photographer: Derek Robinson

4. Plywood is a great low-cost kitchen material. Architect: DMVF | Photographer: Ros Kavanagh

can cause significant delays and, in an industry where time is money, you are the one that will pay. Unless you have building experience or your project is relatively small, you should invest in hiring a respected professional.

Another good way to drive up costs is to add components or change your mind once contracts have been signed. Make sure that all significant elements are agreed and costed before you begin. That means measuring for every socket and light fitting in advance. You can be sure that your builder will charge you for every tiny addition so if this does happen, make sure you agree a price before any extra work is done.

✱ **ARCHITECT'S TIP:** Don't overspend on finishes. Before starting the project, do some research to set realistic cost levels for your finishes. Allow yourself one or two indulgences but try to keep the rest on budget.

COST PLAN

As soon as you start thinking about your renovation or extension, you should begin cost planning. Crack open a spreadsheet and familiarise yourself with its layout and functions as this will be your go-to software for the duration of your project.

The RIAI publish guidelines on average construction and renovation costs in the Republic of Ireland (see *Resources*). The figures are quoted in cost per square metre (sqm) so you can get a rough estimate based on the size of your build. The range of costs vary depending on location – labour and materials tend to be more expensive in urban areas than in rural ones. The level of finish you choose will also greatly affect the costs.

Spending a little of your budget on professional advice at the start of your project can save you money in the long run. If you are using an architect, they will be able to give you guidance on general costs, although you will still need to pinpoint the exact prices of the finishes you want to use. If you don't have an architect or if your project is of a sufficiently large scale, you may want to talk to a quantity surveyor (QS), who can prepare a detailed cost plan for you. Not only will a QS give you a clear understanding of costs, they will also be an independent voice of reason as they are not as invested in the design as you. Extensive, non-standard glazing will look very appealing in drawings but you may feel differently when your QS explains the extensive, non-standard costs!

Even if you employ a professional to estimate costs and manage the build, you will still need to keep a close eye on everything as you are the one that will make the final decisions on what to spend – and, of course, because it's *your* money.

+ EXTENSIVE, NON-STANDARD GLAZING WILL LOOK VERY APPEALING IN DRAWINGS BUT YOU MAY FEEL DIFFERENTLY WHEN YOUR QS EXPLAINS THE EXTENSIVE, NON-STANDARD COSTS!

Architect: DMVF | Photographer: Ros Kavanagh

WHAT IS INCLUDED IN A COST PLAN?

The simple answer to this is that everything goes in the cost plan. It is not just to keep track of what you expect to pay your builder or your architect. It should include everything you spend, from skips, planning fees and light fittings down to every last door handle and screw. There may well be some nasty surprises lying in wait for you but they should never be as a result of poor budgeting.

Costs can broadly be split into two categories:

- The costs of the main contract (typically what you will pay your builder).
- The costs that remain within your control (typically finishes).

BUILD COSTS

Usually, demolition, construction and all associated costs (e.g. insulation, heating, roofing) will be put out to tender to a number of builders and you should receive a detailed breakdown of costs from each one. When you sign a contract with a builder, they usually undertake to provide all the services detailed at the agreed cost.

Make sure to allow for preliminaries in the cost plan. These are items that must be in place before the project can begin but they will not form part of your specification of works, in other words the itemised list of work that you will contract to your builder. The erection of hoarding and scaffolding, skip hire and the installation of site services all fall into this category.

PRIME COST (PC) SUMS

If you are using a standard form contract, PC (prime cost) sums will be included. These are the costs that have not yet been decided and over which you have control. PC sums usually include windows, doors, kitchen (a kitchen designer and/or supplier will look after everything for the kitchen, including taps, sinks, handles, drawers, inserts and kickboards), sanitary ware, tiles, flooring and many other items that you will choose. You will put an estimate for these costs in your builder's contract but the final costs can deviate from this. If there is a difference, it will be borne or recouped by you. Your PC sums list is the first place you will go to cut costs, if necessary, once your project has begun.

CONTINGENCY

A cost plan should also include a contingency of between 5–15 per cent of the total contract amount (including PC sums). It should be double this for period buildings and historic structures. Your contingency fund is an amount set aside for unforeseen costs that are out of your control. You shouldn't touch this money unless there is a problem on site that incurs an extra cost. It is not there to cover a shortfall because, for example, you decided to go with a solid wood parquet floor but had budgeted for laminate. However, if no extra costs arise on the build and your contingency fund remains untouched, then by all means go for the parquet.

FEES AND CONTRIBUTIONS

Don't forget to include all professional fees and any required local authority contributions in your cost plan. There will also be fees for disconnecting and reconnecting utilities. You should factor in the cost of renting and moving as well, if necessary. Be realistic about how long your project will last and keep in mind that it is likely to take longer (and cost more) if you are living in the house.

COST PLAN				
TYPE OF COST	**DESCRIPTION**	**PRICE**	**VAT**	**TOTAL**
BUILD COSTS	Demolition			
	Construction			
	Insulation			
	Electrical			
	Plumbing			
	Heating			
	Roofing			
	Floors			
	Tiling			
	Painting/decorating			
	Carpentry			
	Preliminaries			
PC SUMS	Windows			
	Doors			
	Flooring			
	Kitchen			
	Sanitary ware			
	Tiles			
	Stove			
	Fireplace			
	Ironmongery			

COST PLAN				
TYPE OF COST	**DESCRIPTION**	**PRICE**	**VAT**	**TOTAL**
	Light fittings			
	Paving			
CONTINGENCY	5–15% of contract amount			
PROFESSIONAL FEES	Architect			
	Structural engineer			
	Quantity surveyor			
	Assigned certifier			
	PSDP (health and safety)			
	Mechanical and electrical consultant .			
	Planning and\or conservation specialist			
UTILITY CONNECTIONS	Electricity			
	Gas			
	Water			
LOCAL AUTHORITY	Contribution			
OTHER	Rent			
	Moving costs			
	Kitchen appliances			
	Furniture			
	Carpets, curtains and soft furnishings			
	Landscaping			

MANAGING YOUR MONEY

So, you've got to grips with that spreadsheet and you've filled in every possible potential cost. That's just the beginning. Now you need to track every cent you spend. Whatever your budget, it's likely to be a significant amount and when you're faced with invoices coming from several directions, it's easy to lose sight of the fact that this is *your* money. No matter who else is working on your behalf, it is up to you to ensure that your budget is being spent in the most efficient way possible.

Get a series of quotes for everything you plan to purchase, from your tiles to your main contractor. It probably goes without saying but remember you need to be clear about the difference between an estimate and a quote and never agree to buy a product or service without seeing the total breakdown of costs. Make sure the quote indicates whether or not fitting is included – this can also affect the VAT rate charged.

Check every quote to see if VAT is included and at what rate it is charged. There are two VAT rates in the **Republic of Ireland** that are relevant for most aspects of building work. The higher rate applies to professional services (architectural, engineering, quantity surveying) and individual products, while the lower rate usually applies to work done by builders and other tradespeople. Typically, if your builder or tradesperson orders and installs your product, then VAT is charged on both the product and

From glazing to flooring to stoves and furniture, everything you plan to buy must be costed.
Architect: Broadstone | Photographer: Aisling McCoy

service at the lower rate (subject to certain exemptions). **Northern Ireland** has one VAT rate for both products and services. Make sure to check with the relevant authority for up-to-date rules and rates (see *Resources*).

If you are doing a smaller amount of work and managing it yourself then get as many quotes as you can. Ask friends and ask online for recommendations and prices. Cost materials as well as labour. You may save money by sourcing these yourself but check with your tradespeople as they may be able to avail of trade discounts. And don't underestimate the hassle of having to drive to a distant industrial estate, negotiate with salespeople, order the exact item you need and fit everything into your car.

If you are putting a large project out to tender then you will probably get four to six bids, with costs which can vary hugely. Written quotes should itemise every aspect of work and provide a full breakdown of costs. If all quotes for a certain item are similar and one is way cheaper, ask why. Don't always go for the cheapest quote. Talk to the builders and ask for references to get a feel for the quality of their work and their relationship with clients. You will have to deal with your builder for several weeks or months, so you need to be able to trust each other.

If possible, agree with suppliers and contractors that you will hold back a retention amount (usually 5–10% of the product or service). This is a final payment that will only be released several months after work has finished and all snags have been dealt with. If you use an architect, they will most likely include this retention in your building contract. If you are negotiating directly with a builder or supplier,

All exterior finishes and hard landscaping need to be included in your cost plan.
Architect + Photographer: Alan Bennett Architects

Make sure everything is in working order before the retention is paid.
Architect: DMVF | Photographer: Ruth Maria Murphy

ensure that everyone is clear about when, and under what circumstances, a retention will be released. As with all other agreements, get this in writing.

Beware of deposits – if the company goes bust, you will be left in the lurch. Where a deposit is unavoidable, try to arrange as short a timeline as possible. Similarly, try not to pay for building works in advance. Arrange payments to your builder regularly for works completed in arrears.

Ensure that all finances are in place before you start work. I've heard of one horror story where the builder walked off site as he had not been paid because the bank required further paperwork. If your loan or mortgage is ready to go, make sure that drawdown will occur in time to pay your builder at agreed dates.

Finally, keep a file of all your quotes, invoices and receipts. Put all instructions to your builder in writing and hold on to a copy. And keep updating that spreadsheet.

QUANTITY SURVEYOR'S TOP TIPS FOR STAYING OUT OF TROUBLE

1. Get your structure right now and worry about your finishes later.

2. Do your cost plan before the detailed design stage – there's no point in designing features you can't afford.

3. Be realistic – don't say you'll spend €5,000 on a kitchen when all the kitchens you love cost €25,000.

4. If you don't have a professional overseeing your build, do consider getting a quantity surveyor to manage payments to your builder so your QS can ensure that all required work is completed first.

5. Make sure you have specified all works in the contract, otherwise variations can be contentious and costly.

6. If you have an architect, communicate all your decisions to them and let them talk to the builder. If you are dealing directly with your builder, make sure you discuss the cost of all changes before you go ahead with them.

7. Do not start any job of any size without a contract.

8. Don't fall out with your builder over minor disagreements. An adversarial relationship will make the build very stressful for all parties. If you end the project on a good note, your builder is more likely to come back and fix things, even after you've paid the retention.

Declan Doyle, Quantity Surveyor

GRANTS AND SCHEMES

There are often tax incentives for people renovating or extending their homes. It's worth checking government websites to see if anything is available. The incentives can change rapidly but the last couple of decades have seen significant schemes (see *Resources*).

There are also often energy rebates and grants available for home insulation and heating upgrades. The Sustainable Energy Authority of Ireland has more information for **Republic of Ireland** residents, while those in **Northern Ireland** can check with the Northern Ireland Housing Executive.

If your home is a protected structure in the Republic of Ireland, there may be funding available from the Irish Georgian Society. For listed buildings in Northern Ireland, check your local authority to see if any grants are available (see *Resources*).

THERE ARE OFTEN TAX INCENTIVES FOR PEOPLE RENOVATING OR EXTENDING THEIR HOMES.

Architect: DMVF | Photographer: Ruth Maria Murphy

1950s SEMI-DETACHED DORMER BUNGALOW

WHO LIVES HERE:
Nico Dowling, his wife, Daniela, and their two children

LOCATION:
Rathfarnham, Dublin 14

PROJECT:
Complete renovation and extension

This two-storey addition to a dormer bungalow both compliments and contradicts the proportions of the original house.
All images in case study: Architect: DMVF | Photographer: Ruth Maria Murphy

Front view of original house.

THE PROPERTY

Nico and Daniela rented their house for eight years before buying it, four years ago.
'It had been quite rundown so the plan was always to do a big job on it,' says Nico.
It sits on a large corner site so they had plenty of options.
'We wanted to double the size of the house, to have one big open-plan living space, and we wanted it to be contemporary.'

THE DESIGN

The couple took a while to work out exactly what they wanted in terms of style.
'We didn't have a strong opinion on that at the start. Our architect really helped us figure out that part of it.'
Their architect introduced the idea of an L-shaped extension, which would allow for garden on both sides and not have as big an impact on the outdoor space as Nico had feared. The original house would be left largely unchanged.

THE COSTS

Delighted with the design and with planning permission secured, the couple put the job out to tender. While they were concerned about costs, they weren't expecting the quotes to be so significantly over-budget.

'Initially, we thought we wouldn't be able to do it and we'd have to go back to the drawing board but our architect was brilliant. He said, let's just slash it and see how far we can get.'

Nico concentrated on cutting features that wouldn't change the footprint of the design.

'We cut all our landscaping and we cut a zinc roof – that was a massive saving. We put tiles on in the end and we were way happier with how that looked.'

By removing work that could be done at a later stage, Nico managed to get costs under control. And, as there were no surprises on the build, the contingency was available for some of the interior design that had been taken out of the contract.

'We were so happy that we didn't have to lose any space in the end. The only thing we regret is that we didn't put underfloor heating in the old part of the house.'

Rear view of original house.

Original kitchen.

Original house plan.

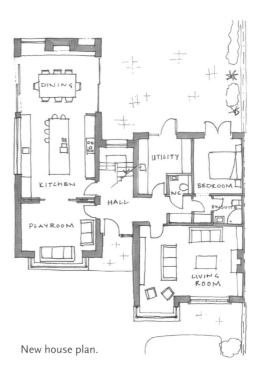

New house plan.

THE BEST BITS

There's no particular spot that the couple favours; it's the overall effect they love.

'I love the feel, the space, the light, the openness of the house,' says Nico. 'When the weather's nice, we open both the doors and there's a breeze blowing through the house that almost makes it feel like you're abroad.'

Given that Nico and Daniela lived in the house for over ten years before they renovated, they appreciate it all the more now.

'It was a bit of a dump before. It was always cold and nothing worked properly so even having a shower that works is amazing. I constantly just stop and go: "This is great; I can't believe this is our house!"'

'WHEN THE WEATHER'S NICE, WE OPEN BOTH THE DOORS AND THERE'S A BREEZE BLOWING THROUGH THE HOUSE THAT ALMOST MAKES IT FEEL LIKE YOU'RE ABROAD.'

5 PLANNING

IT IS USUALLY BETTER TO GO AHEAD
AND DESIGN THE HOME YOU WANT
FIRST AND THEN LOOK AT WHETHER
OR NOT YOU ARE REQUIRED TO GO
THROUGH THE PLANNING PROCESS.

This extension harmonises with the style, materials and character of the original house, as often required by the planning authority.
Architect: DMVF | Photographer: Infinity Media

UNDERSTANDING THE PROCESS

Designing your dream home takes vision and ambition; getting it built requires diligence and practicality. As with your costs, planning laws and guidelines must be observed and incorporated into your plans. These laws control and structure the scope of any development, and in doing so protect individuals, neighbourhoods and the environment. Development is, in principle, viewed positively by planning authorities and their aim is to support homeowners to build and improve their homes. So, don't be afraid of the planning process but do stick to the rules to give yourself the best chance of success.

PLANNING PERMISSION AND EXEMPTIONS

The first question everyone thinking about a build asks is, 'Will I need planning permission?' The simple answer is that, yes, you need permission for any demolition, building or alteration of a property (or a significant change of use of that property) unless it is specifically exempted. In the **Republic of Ireland**, residential extensions under 40 square metres (sqm) are generally exempt from planning permission, subject to a number of restrictions. In **Northern Ireland**, there are restrictions on depth for a rear extension (4 metres (m) for a detached house and 3 m for a semi-detached house or terrace) and width for a side extension (4 m or no more than half the width of the original house), along with a number of other conditions. Always check with your local authority for up to date legislation and guidelines before you begin the design process.

It's important that this arbitrary figure of 40 sqm or 4 m in depth, which applies equally to a small cottage or a large detached house, should not be an overriding concern, especially if you are undertaking extensive work. It is usually better to go ahead and design the home you want first and then look at whether or not you are required to go through the planning process. If you are building a new home, you will need planning permission, regardless of the proposed size of your house. If you are planning an extension to an existing home, you will need to weigh up the pros and cons of an application, especially if you are currently living elsewhere.

Legislation and regulations can change at any time and all the information included here is only a general guide. You need to clarify with your local authority and/or a suitably-qualified professional that your proposed works are compliant with all relevant legislation and regulations within your jurisdiction. It is a good idea to get this in writing before starting work.

Applying for planning permission does take time and it can add an extra layer of stress to your project but, in the end, it could be the difference between building a home you like and making the home you love.

REPUBLIC OF IRELAND

PLANNING INFORMATION AND ADVICE

A planning application is made to your local authority, who will decide to grant or refuse permission. Its decision will be based on planning legislation and in keeping with its own local development plan, a document that sets out the policies and objectives for development in each area. The Department of Housing, Planning and Local Government produces a number of free guides, which cover a whole range of issues from planning requirements to how to lodge an application, appeals, building controls and enforcement (see *Resources*).

Some amount of development is usually allowed in urban areas, subject to planning permission.
Architect: Broadstone | Photographer: Aisling McCoy

The planning section of your local authority's website will have more detailed information specific to your area, including the local development plan. You should also have a look at other planning applications from your area online to see what decisions were made and the reasons given. This is a good way of assessing what sort of development is possible and what is likely to be refused. Any planning precedents in your area and, in particular, on your street can be included in your application. The drawings submitted with other planning applications can also be a great source of inspiration for your own designs, especially if the houses are of a similar style and size.

While the published information is useful, it can be quite general so it's a good idea to talk to an architect for more specific advice about your particular plans. You can also organise a free pre-planning meeting with your local authority, which will give you a better idea of what's required. This is most useful for one-off houses in the countryside where development may be restricted, as opposed to urban areas where some amount of development is usually acceptable.

✱ **ARCHITECT'S TIP:** Applications for planning permission are free to view online. Have a look at application forms, paperwork, drawings, decisions, planners' reports and other documents. Most local authorities allow you to search by keywords, such as name and address, or by map.

Planning applications in your area will give you a good idea of what is considered acceptable, and can also be a great source of inspiration. | Architect: Anima & John McLaughlin Architects | Photographer: Alice Clancy

EXEMPTED DEVELOPMENT

If you're planning an extension in the Republic of Ireland, you'll hear a lot about the 40 sqm exemption. This is set out in planning law so it does not vary from one local authority to another. As mentioned in *Preparation*, if your extension is less than 40 sqm to the rear of the house and maintains at least 25 sqm of garden space, then you are not likely to need planning permission. Up to 20 sqm of your allowance can be built at first floor level if your house is detached and up to 12 sqm if it is semi-detached or terraced (subject to a number of dimensional constraints and other conditions).

Keep in mind that the 40 sqm is for all developments, including garage conversions, so if you're thinking of converting your garage or you have an existing extension built after the introduction of planning legislation in 1963, then the size needs to be factored in. There are many other restrictions on exempted development, and some of these can depend on your particular proposal and circumstances, so make sure to consult with a professional or your local authority before starting your extension or conversion.

One big exception to the provisions above is if your property is a protected structure or is located in an Architectural Conservation Area. In that case full planning permission is usually required for any development or conversion and it is best to use an architect and builder who are familiar with protected structures and the associated planning issues.

Don't start any work until you have confirmation, in writing, from a suitably-qualified person or from your local authority, that planning permission is not required.

✱ ARCHITECT'S TIP: Check your drainage before you start the design process. Write to Irish Water and ask for a copy of the public drainage and water-main map for your site. The water main is a pipe carrying the supply of water to the house, while public drains are pipes that drain away surface water (rainwater) and foul water. If there is a public drain or water main running through or close to your site, this may curtail development. You also need to know the existing drainage layout on your site and to find out where and how you connect to the main drain or to your septic tank. This information should be included in your planning application.

THE PLANNING PROCESS

The planning process typically takes about twelve weeks from the day you lodge your application. However, this is a best-case scenario and you should not plan your build around this timescale. Delays can be caused by a number of factors, often beyond your control (for example, a planning appeal by a third party), so try not to get despondent if you are hit by one of them. If your design is reasonable and complies with the local development plan then you should be in a good position to get planning permission or approval subject to conditions.

✱ ARCHITECT'S TIP: Take your time. For larger projects, factor in a minimum of twelve weeks' preparation to allow your architect to prepare the drawings and documents required for planning permission. This may seem like a long time but in reality, this is where you commit to most of your big decisions and to your budget. Think about all of the options on the table as the decisions you make could be with you for a lifetime.

For one-off houses in the country, outline permission can be useful to make sure the planning authority agrees with your proposal in principle. | Architect: Broadstone | Photographer: Aidan Monaghan

There are two types of planning permission: outline permission and full permission. You may want to apply for outline permission first, particularly if you are hoping to build a one-off house in the countryside. This will tell you if the planning authority agrees with your proposal in principle, before you go to the trouble of developing your plans in detail. However, you will still need full permission before you can start work so, for most urban development, people skip straight to the real deal.

You can only make a planning application if you have sufficient legal interest in the property. If you are in the process of purchasing your home or if you rent it then you need to include written permission from the owner with your application.

Before you submit your application, you need to publish your intention in an approved local newspaper (your local authority can advise on this) and erect a notice on the site. Details on what should be included in these notices are available from your local authority and your application should be received within two weeks of each notice being published and displayed. Copies of both of these notices should be included in your application, along with a plan showing the position of the site notice, the application form, a location map, a site or layout plan, other plans, elevations and sections and the appropriate fee. You may also need further documentation so check in advance with your local authority. As most homeowners do not have the expertise needed to prepare the drawings and other documents needed for the application, hiring a professional to oversee this stage will most likely save you time and money in the long run.

TYPICAL TIMESCALE

OBSERVATION PERIOD
Once your application has been received by your local authority, a five week observation period follows, during which anyone can make an observation (usually an objection). Your site notice has to remain in place for these five weeks.

DECISION
Three weeks after that, and provided no further information is requested, you should receive a decision of intention to grant planning permission.

APPEAL PERIOD
You then have to wait a further four weeks during which you or any of those who have commented on your application can appeal the decision to An Bord Pleanála. An independent body, An Bord Pleanála decides on planning appeals from local authorities around the country. Statutory bodies can also appeal without having made an observation.

PERMISSION
Assuming that there are no appeals, then the final grant of permission will issue and you should receive this in due course from your local authority.

POSSIBLE DELAYS
There are a number of outcomes to the planning process that can result in delays. The five listed here are the most typical.

1. AN INVALID APPLICATION
If your application is incomplete or invalid, it will be returned to you with the fee. Common reasons for this are if it is not received within the required timeframe or the site plan is missing dimensions. This can add a couple of weeks to your timeline.

2. A REQUEST FOR ADDITIONAL INFORMATION
The case officer in charge of your application may request further information before they can make a decision. This adds approximately four weeks to the planning process, and you also have to allow for the time it takes you to prepare the additional documentation.

3. A THIRD PARTY APPEAL
An Bord Pleanála aims to make planning appeal decisions within eighteen weeks of receiving them. However, this should be viewed as the minimum waiting period as in reality it can take several weeks more during busy periods.

4. UNACCEPTABLE CONDITIONS
Your local authority can attach conditions to your planning permission. For example, you may be asked to omit a window or a second storey. If these conditions fundamentally change the vision you have for your home, you may want to appeal the decision yourself.

5. REFUSAL OF PERMISSION
A refusal gives you one of three options, all of which incur considerable delays: you can appeal the decision, you can redesign your plans in line with the planner's assessment and submit a new application, or you can start from scratch and stay within the boundaries of exempted development. Only the third option offers any guarantee that you will be able to go ahead with your project.

PLANNING PROCESS

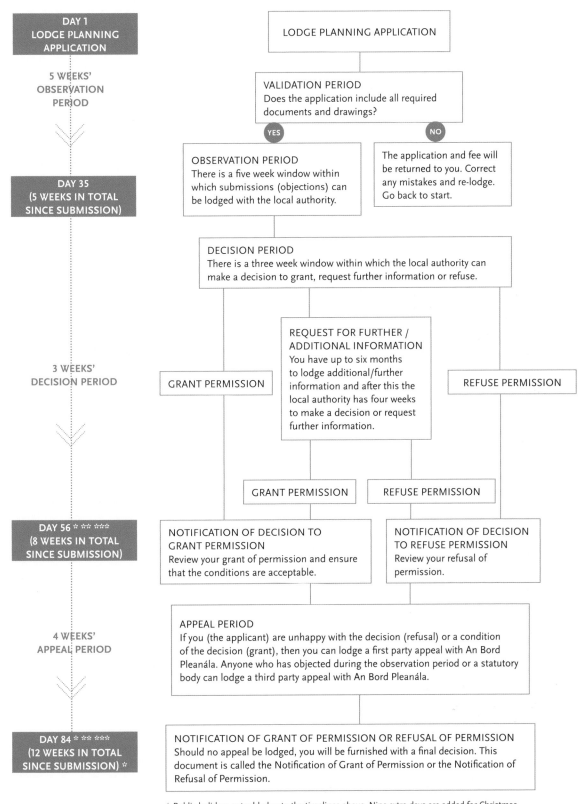

DAY 1
LODGE PLANNING APPLICATION

5 WEEKS' OBSERVATION PERIOD

DAY 35
(5 WEEKS IN TOTAL SINCE SUBMISSION)

3 WEEKS' DECISION PERIOD

DAY 56 ✳ ✳✳ ✳✳✳
(8 WEEKS IN TOTAL SINCE SUBMISSION)

4 WEEKS' APPEAL PERIOD

DAY 84 ✳ ✳✳ ✳✳✳
(12 WEEKS IN TOTAL SINCE SUBMISSION) ✳

LODGE PLANNING APPLICATION

VALIDATION PERIOD
Does the application include all required documents and drawings?

YES — NO

OBSERVATION PERIOD
There is a five week window within which submissions (objections) can be lodged with the local authority.

The application and fee will be returned to you. Correct any mistakes and re-lodge. Go back to start.

DECISION PERIOD
There is a three week window within which the local authority can make a decision to grant, request further information or refuse.

REQUEST FOR FURTHER / ADDITIONAL INFORMATION
You have up to six months to lodge additional/further information and after this the local authority has four weeks to make a decision or request further information.

GRANT PERMISSION

REFUSE PERMISSION

GRANT PERMISSION

REFUSE PERMISSION

NOTIFICATION OF DECISION TO GRANT PERMISSION
Review your grant of permission and ensure that the conditions are acceptable.

NOTIFICATION OF DECISION TO REFUSE PERMISSION
Review your refusal of permission.

APPEAL PERIOD
If you (the applicant) are unhappy with the decision (refusal) or a condition of the decision (grant), then you can lodge a first party appeal with An Bord Pleanála. Anyone who has objected during the observation period or a statutory body can lodge a third party appeal with An Bord Pleanála.

NOTIFICATION OF GRANT OF PERMISSION OR REFUSAL OF PERMISSION
Should no appeal be lodged, you will be furnished with a final decision. This document is called the Notification of Grant of Permission or the Notification of Refusal of Permission.

✳ Public holidays get added onto the timelines above. Nine extra days are added for Christmas.
✳✳ Allow a minimum of four or more weeks if further/additional information is requested.
✳✳✳ Processing of paperwork by your local authority may add to this timeline.

PLANNING APPEALS

In the diagram on the previous page, you can see that if your local authority refuses permission or if you cannot live with the conditions attached to your grant of permission, you may appeal the decision to An Bord Pleanála. Here, your application will be looked at anew. An appeal should not be taken on lightly, however, as the decision made by the board is final – it is the end of the line. Even if you and your architect are confident that your plans are reasonable and that there is plenty of precedent in your local area, you may want to get the opinion of a planning consultant before deciding on your next move. For example, you might conclude that it would be better or quicker to redesign your plans and submit a fresh application to the local authority. If you decide to go ahead with the appeal, it's worth considering hiring a planning consultant to prepare your application, depending on the complexity of the project. As you've come this far, you need to pull out all the stops to get your proposal over the line.

Your appeal must include your name and address, details of the proposed development, the name of the local authority, the planning register number, your grounds of appeal with all supporting material and arguments, and your fee.

If the appeal has been initiated by a third party (most likely someone who objected to the original application), you will get a chance to make a submission in response. The appellant will then also get a chance to reply to your answer.

A planning inspector will visit your property in due course and report back to the board, which will then make a decision to grant or refuse permission.

I'm not going to lie to you, a planning appeal can be hugely stressful, especially if you are paying rent elsewhere while you wait out the five to six months a decision can take. The creeping costs and the fear of the unknown can keep you awake at night, even if your planning consultant has assured you that you're a shoe-in. The pain is soon forgotten, however, when you finally move into your beautiful new home, so bear with it and have faith.

All planning woes are soon forgotten when you move into your beautiful new home so keep calm and keep your eyes on the prize. | Architect: DMVF | Photographer: Ruth Maria Murphy

If you are planning a one-off house, a pre-application meeting with a planning officer can give you an idea of your chance of success. | Architect: DMVF | Photographer: Paul Tierney

NORTHERN IRELAND

PLANNING INFORMATION AND ADVICE

Planning applications are made to the Local Planning Office at your local authority, which you can find online (see *Resources*). Advice and leaflets are also available. Your first step should be to call and ask for advice on whether or not you need to apply for planning permission. If it sounds like your work falls under permitted development, you can apply for a Certificate of Lawfulness and this takes approximately 4–6 weeks to process. This is not a necessity but it can be useful if you or your architect are not certain about the status of your plans. If a planning officer thinks you do need planning permission, then ask to be sent an application pack. You can view information on the various application forms online and search for planning applications by keyword, application reference, postcode or by a single line of an address. Have a look through applications in your area to see what decisions have been made and the reasons given. This is both a good way of assessing what is permissible and a great source of inspiration for your own designs.

You may also apply for a pre-application discussion with a planning officer. This is especially useful for one-off houses as you can find out if development is allowed in principle, before you go to the trouble of developing your designs.

While all of this information is useful, it is no substitute for professional advice. To give yourself the best chance of success, you should get an architect to prepare drawings and supporting documentation for your application. If your project is big or complex, you may also want to talk to a planning consultant, who can guide you through any potential pitfalls.

PERMITTED DEVELOPMENT

Planning permission is not required in Northern Ireland as long as work stays strictly within the limits set out by the *Planning (General Permitted Development) Order (Northern Ireland) 2015*. Under these rules, you can build a single-storey rear extension up to 4 m in depth for a detached house and 3 m for a semi-detached or terraced house. If you're building more than one storey then the limit is 3 m, regardless of the type of house. A side extension should not exceed 4 m in height or be wider than half the width of the original house. In addition, the floor area of all extensions and buildings (excluding the original house) should not be greater than half of the area of the property. In other words, you cannot cover more than half the land around your house with extensions and you must include sheds or other outbuildings when calculating this coverage.

If your house has been extended previously since 1973 or if you have any other buildings within the boundary of the property, then you will have to factor those into your calculations. There are a number of other restrictions, so make sure to check online and talk to your Local Area Planning Office before you begin any work.

If you live in a listed building then you will most likely need Listed Building Consent for any work you intend to do. Contact your local authority for advice on this and consider using an architect who has experience with period buildings.

This eighteenth-century mill house has been renovated with natural materials to balance character and contemporary living. | Interior Architecture: Maria Fenlon | Photographer: Sean & Yvette

THE PLANNING PROCESS

There are two types of planning permission you can apply for in Northern Ireland – outline and full planning permission. Outline planning grants permission in principle, subject to certain design restrictions and conditions. If you are planning a new build, it can be useful to know that some development is permissible before you go to the trouble of developing your plans in full. However, the information required for an outline application is so detailed that most homeowners decide to make a full planning application instead.

Generally, a planning application should include five copies of the application form and five copies of the supporting documentation – site layout/block plans, floor plans, elevations, location plans (preferably Ordnance Survey) and the relevant fee. The completed application should be sent to the Local Area Planning Office at your local authority. There may be further documentation required, so make sure to check with your local authority.

This extension has a minimal impact on neighbouring properties. | Architect: David Flynn | Photographer: Barbara Corsico

TYPICAL TIMESCALE

Unlike the Republic of Ireland, there are no set timescales for the review of planning applications in Northern Ireland. There are anticipated timeframes, but these can vary greatly from council to council and can range from two to three months to twelve months and beyond, depending on the size and scale of the development.

When you have submitted a full planning application, there are five stages it can go through before a decision is reached:

STAGE 1

Once your application is received and processed, the Local Area Planning Office will place an advertisement in a local paper and write to neighbours to invite comments. Any other relevant bodies, such as the Roads Service, will be consulted. This typically takes three to four weeks. If an objection is received, this can delay the process.

STAGE 2

Your application will then proceed to an internal planning review. An assigned case officer will visit your site and prepare a report, which will be considered by a Development Management Group meeting. An opinion on the application will then be formed. If the application is simple in nature and scale, straightforward and non-contentious, then a decision to grant permission may be streamlined and sent straight to the local council. Provided there is no formal request from a councillor to bring the application before the local council, the decision will be circulated to all interested parties. This stage usually takes from four to eight weeks.

STAGE 3

If your application does not meet the criteria for streamlining, it will be sent to the local council and they will consider your proposal and the opinion of the Development Management Group.

PLANNING PROCESS

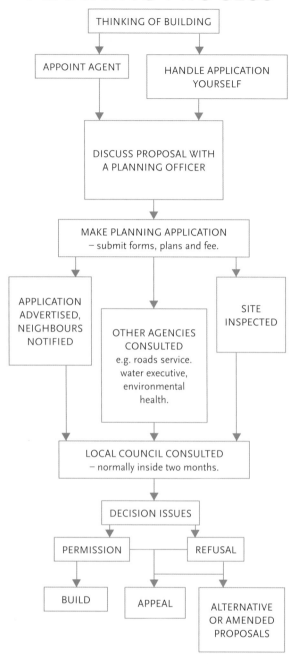

THINKING OF BUILDING

APPOINT AGENT

HANDLE APPLICATION YOURSELF

DISCUSS PROPOSAL WITH A PLANNING OFFICER

MAKE PLANNING APPLICATION
– submit forms, plans and fee.

APPLICATION ADVERTISED, NEIGHBOURS NOTIFIED

OTHER AGENCIES CONSULTED
e.g. roads service. water executive, environmental health.

SITE INSPECTED

LOCAL COUNCIL CONSULTED
– normally inside two months.

DECISION ISSUES

PERMISSION

REFUSAL

BUILD

APPEAL

ALTERNATIVE OR AMENDED PROPOSALS

STAGE 4

Your application will be presented and reviewed at a formal local council planning meeting, where a chief planner and councillors are present. This happens within around two to four weeks, depending on when the meeting (which is usually monthly) is scheduled.

STAGE 5

If the council has no objections then the application will be approved. If permission is refused, then you and your team can ask for representation at the council meeting. You put forward your case in the hope that any amendments you propose will reverse the decision. If the application is still refused then an appeal to the Planning Appeals Commission is the only remaining option.

PLANNING APPEALS

If you have been refused planning permission or if there have been conditions attached to your grant of permission that you just can't live with, you can appeal the decision to the Planning Appeals Commission (see *Resources*). Appeals can only be made by or on behalf of the person who made the application for planning permission – there is no third party right of appeal as in the Republic of Ireland. However, anyone who commented on the original application can make a representation to the Planning Appeals Commission.

You must lodge an appeal within four months of the date of notification of the local council's decision. Appeals can be made online, by post or in person at the Commission's offices.

Householder appeals are submitted using written representations. The planning inspector will consider written evidence from you, the local authority and anyone else who has an interest in the appeal. The inspector will also visit the site and a written decision notice is then prepared several weeks later, detailing whether or not you've been granted permission. When it is issued, all those with an interest in the application are notified.

THE NEIGHBOURS

Many of the delays that can arise during the planning process can be avoided with careful preparation. However, the one thing that you cannot control is how other people will react to your proposal. Depending on the size and scope of your build, it may have a noticeable effect on neighbouring properties and the construction phase can cause noise and dust. In urban areas in particular, most development has some impact on its surroundings. Extensions can cause overshadowing and this may cause friction in the most neighbourly of relationships, even if the project is exempted from planning permission or there is precedence in the area for the redesign.

It is good manners to talk to your neighbours before you start any work. Most people are resistant to change being thrust upon them so go in with your eyes open and be prepared for possible conflict. Listen to their concerns and make compromises if you want, but don't be unduly pressured into making changes you will not be happy with in the long run. This is your home and you will be the one living in it. If it's exempted development, it is already considered reasonable and if not, the local authority will make that decision.

In **Northern Ireland**, it is only someone affected by a development who can comment on a planning application, whereas in the **Republic of Ireland**, anyone, anywhere can have their say. So, don't take it personally if someone objects. While a planner will take on board any observations, in theory objections should not materially compromise the outcome unless there are valid grounds for them. Similarly, your application is not less likely to succeed based on how many comments are received. In practice, it seems that objections can sometimes result in minor conditions being attached to a grant of permission, but they are unlikely to influence the decision to grant or refuse permission.

It is important to keep in mind, as a neighbour yourself, that those living close to you may one day build a bigger and badder extension than your own. When designing your home and your garden, imagine how a patio or a side window will look with a 3 m wall abutting it, or how a balcony may feel with another just a few metres away. If it's an option, build that patio out further or keep it to the back of the house instead of the side. Consider roof lights as well as windows. Never assume that other people won't remodel and even if *they* don't, who knows what their successors will do?

✱ **ARCHITECT'S TIP:** Try to stay calm. Just as you are entitled to make a planning application, your neighbours are entitled to object to it. Your local authority is used to being an arbiter between parties and they will make a decision that considers existing residents and residences as well as your wants or needs. Try to allow plenty of time for the planning process in your build schedule as this will take much of the stress out of it.

Architect: David Flynn | Photographer: Barbara Corsico

1960s BUNGALOW

WHO LIVES HERE:
Anne Flood, her husband and two children

LOCATION:
Dunshaughlin, County Meath

PROJECT:
Substantial renovation and extension

Front view of original house.

This 1960s bungalow was opened up to the front and the rear to allow light to flow through the house all day.
All images in case study: Architect: DMVF | Photographer: Paul Tierney

THE PROPERTY

In 2008, Anne and her husband bought a small bungalow on a large site in County Meath.

'What attracted us to the site was all the mature trees and the privacy they gave the house,' says Anne. 'We were more drawn to the site than the house itself.'

The brief was to provide a family home for the couple and their two young kids, that would adapt as the children grew. Anne wanted it to be full of light and to open up to the front of the house, which was south-facing, and to the back where the children would play.

'We also wanted a home office and a guest bedroom at ground floor level as we regularly have friends and family staying over.'

The house needed to undergo a substantial renovation that would replace most of the features of the original building.

'Almost everything was constructed new, apart from some of the external walls.'

THE PLANNING

Anne and her husband were slightly apprehensive going into the planning process. **'The design was very contemporary in nature and it wasn't the typical dormer bungalow that is usually constructed in the area.'** However, they were shocked when it got an outright refusal from Meath County Council. **'The reason they gave was the complicated nature of the roof but our architect advised that the roof was actually fairly simple and not as complicated as roofs in the dormer bungalows you see everywhere. There was a rationale behind the roof design and the site was shielded from the road by tall, mature trees.'** The couple's initial response was to go back to the drawing board but they weren't happy with the changes that had to be made to address the planning department's concerns.

'The result looked very traditional and there was nothing special about it, so that made up our minds to lodge the appeal, even though it would delay the project by five months.' In the end, An Bord Pleanála agreed that the roof wasn't overly complicated and threw out the county council's decision.

'We were delighted and so relieved. It was definitely worth it, but we'd never have had the nerve to go through with the appeal without the support of our architect.'

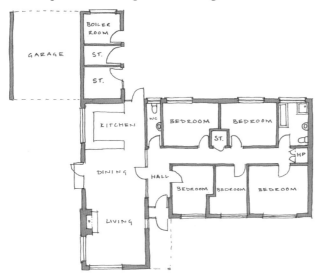

Original house plan.

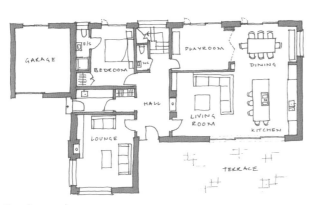

New house plan.

Rear view of original house.

Original living room.

THE BEST BITS

Anne loves the sense of space throughout the house and the large open-plan living/kitchen/dining room in which the family spends most of its time.

'The space opens to the front and the back so we get daylight all day long, and you can see the kids no matter where they are in the garden.'

She also appreciates how well the space has been designed to suit their needs.

'The house can fit loads of visitors, yet it never feels too large for the four of us as a family.'

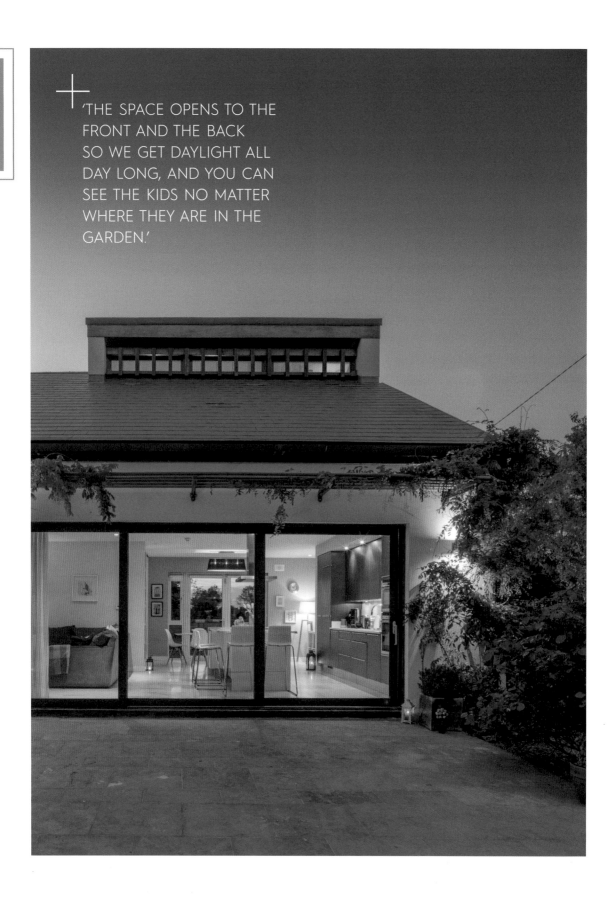

'THE SPACE OPENS TO THE FRONT AND THE BACK SO WE GET DAYLIGHT ALL DAY LONG, AND YOU CAN SEE THE KIDS NO MATTER WHERE THEY ARE IN THE GARDEN.'

6 TENDERING

THE MORE DETAIL
YOU INCLUDE IN
YOUR TENDER
DOCUMENTS, THE
MORE ACCURATE
AND SPECIFIC THE
QUOTES WILL BE.

This large, one-off house in County Kildare was designed to maximise views of the nearby paddock.
Architect: Broadstone | Photographer: Paul Tierney

WHAT IS TENDERING?

Tendering is the process by which contractors are invited to provide quotes for specific works or services. Whether you are looking for a builder to complete your entire construction project or you are getting a price for a new kitchen or windows, it is always a good idea to seek bids from a number of suppliers. The idea is that each company is pricing from the same tender package so the quotes you receive can be compared on an itemised basis. The more detail you include in your tender documents, the more accurate and specific the quotes will be. It's important to remember that it won't cost you to take out elements at a later stage but you can be pretty sure it will cost you to add them in.

The success of the tender process really depends on how much time and preparation you put into it. Now that you have reached this stage, after you've prepared your drawings, estimated your budget costs and received planning permission, you may be tempted to rush headlong into the build. Stop. Breathe. Relax. Your project is going to happen, but how it happens is contingent on how well you manage this part of the process.

If you are using an architect to manage your build then they will guide you through the tendering process, preparing all documents and drawings, and liaising with builders. Your job will be to do as much research as possible so you can make decisions about the finishes and fittings to be included in the tender – your windows, kitchen, floor finishes, tiles, fitted wardrobes, your carpentry requirements, electrical and plumbing layouts and heating may all need to be considered at this stage.

If you are self-managing a renovation or build, then read this chapter carefully. This is the stage where you commit your own money to the project and, without the benefit of experience, you are taking on a greater level of risk. To try to minimise this, it is a good idea to enlist the help of an architect or a quantity surveyor to guide you through the tender process. However, if you do choose to go it alone, you should revisit your costs and increase your contingency fund to allow for the greater unknowns. Bear in mind also that you will still need a suitably-qualified building professional to sign off on the finished work, to ensure that it's in compliance with planning and building regulations.

It's also a good idea to show drawings and literature to window, door and kitchen contractors for pricing at this stage, as it will give you a better idea of where you stand financially. That way, if the tender prices are higher than expected, you can cut back on your window and kitchen specifications as necessary.

THE MORE YOU
KNOW ABOUT ALL
THE POTENTIAL
COSTS AND
EVENTUALITIES, THE
MORE CONTROL YOU
WILL HAVE ONCE THE
PROJECT STARTS.

Older buildings, in particular, can have significant hidden costs.
Interior Architecture: Maria Fenlon | Photographer: Gareth Byrne

PRE-TENDER INVESTIGATIONS

Any existing building can have significant hidden problems, which could mean you are hit with higher costs. Without a full advance investigation, you may end up discovering these problems mid-build and have to pay for them as extras.

There are a number of investigations a professional can do which may help to identify areas requiring attention before you prepare your tender documents.

1. TRIAL PITS

These are holes or pits in the ground that can be dug out and used to inspect existing foundations, identify the water table and soil conditions, and locate below-ground drainage or services. The tests are normally carried out by the builder, under a professional's instruction.

2. OPENING UP WORKS

This is when you remove or excavate parts of the building to identify what might be going on behind the surface. You could remove plaster to reveal a window head to check on its condition,

or remove part of a ceiling to inspect the length of a beam overhead. You may also want to lift a floorboard or two to check for rot. You can also check for damp using a damp meter.

3. DRAINAGE SURVEY

A camera survey of your below-ground drainage by a specialist drainage company should tell you the condition and location of your drains. It is important to check that the locations of drainage runs and inspection chambers do not interfere with new construction works.

4. ASBESTOS SURVEY

Many older buildings are likely to contain some form of asbestos. A survey by a specialist will allow you to identify areas of your home that need asbestos removal. Asbestos needs to be carefully and correctly removed and this can have a cost.

5. CONDITIONS SURVEY

You may also want to have the rest of the property surveyed to check the roof, walls, floors and foundations. A party wall survey may also be advisable.

✱ **ARCHITECT'S TIP:** If your property is similar to your neighbour's house, then it might be worthwhile asking them if there are any hidden secrets that you should be aware of. For example, they may have carried out an extension and found that the ground wasn't ideal or that there were almost no foundations under the walls of the older part of the house!

TENDER PACKAGE

The key to a successful tendering process is to make sure your builders have the correct information to use as a basis for their quotes. Whether you are looking to hire one contractor or several separate tradespeople, the same principle applies: all work needs to be listed, described and drawn in as much detail as possible. A typical tender package contains:

- A cover letter that specifies your contract
- Construction drawings
- A written specification of works
- Any other relevant documents

It is essential to include details of every single aspect of the work to be completed – if you don't, it leaves you open to having to accept any price proposed for omitted jobs once contracts have been signed or, worse still, when the work has already been done. The more you agree at the start of a project, the less room there is for dispute at the end.

CONTRACTS

The tender documents don't contain the contract itself. A cover letter is included, which contains an invitation to contract. This simply describes the contract to be used.

Standard building contracts have been developed by professional bodies over many years and include tried and tested clauses that deal with issues that arise throughout the construction process. The completed contract sets out the terms under which construction is to be carried out, the basis for payments, the time scale, and penalties (if any) for failure to comply with terms of the contract.

The Royal Institute of the Architects of Ireland in the Republic of Ireland and the Joint Contracts Tribunal in Northern Ireland have a number of standard form contracts that set out the rules, terms and conditions for what the builder, consultants and client will do, and when they will do it. They have evolved over the years to deal with problems and disputes that have occurred in the past and are adjusted from time to time to reflect changes in legislation and case law.

RIAI and JCT form contracts are designed to be administered by an architect when engaging a main contractor. If you are managing the build yourself and using a single contractor, the standard form contract contains plenty of useful information you can draw on to develop your own contract. You should detail exactly what work is to be done and when payment will be due. It's also a good idea to have a finish date and specific penalties for missing this. If you are employing the services of many different tradespeople, you will need to have a contract with each one, covering both parties' responsibilities.

An architect usually acts as the contract administrator, implementing and monitoring it. They are the impartial arbitrator, checking the quality of work and issuing payment certificates. It is very useful to have professional help at this stage as an architect will have the experience and clout to keep your builder in check and won't sign off on any job that is not up to scratch. And, with future work and recommendations in the balance, it's in everyone's interest to do the best job they can.

The contract is also the place to set the retention amount, the percentage of payment to be held back until after all work is completed. This money is paid to the contractor after the 'defects liability period' (DLP) or 'rectification period'. However, some of this amount can be deducted in certain circumstances, for example, if the builder has failed to make good on defects. You should also specify the start and end date of the project and any damages to be paid to the client because of delays caused by the contractor.

TENDER DRAWING

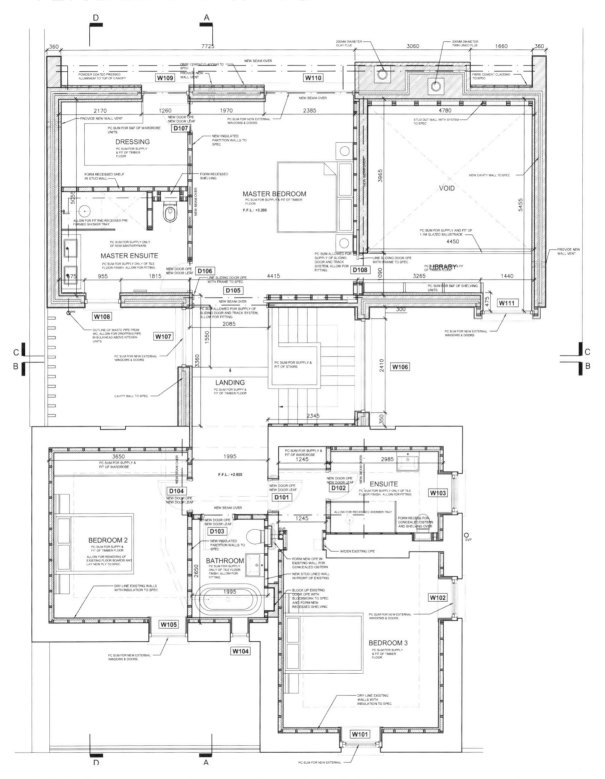

Tender drawings have much more detail than regular floor plans so don't be tempted to use floor plans instead.

CONSTRUCTION DRAWINGS

Construction drawings contain all the necessary structural, engineering, materials, mechanical, electrical and plumbing details for building and finishing a project. Planning drawings rarely show this level of detail so don't be tempted to use them instead. You will need to decide on all finishes, electrical and plumbing layouts, heating, the shape and size of your kitchen units, insulation strategy and any carpentry, in order to complete your construction drawings. Your architect will also include information on all technical matters – foundations, boundary treatments, drainage and anything else that's relevant.

Don't underestimate the amount of work that goes into construction drawings – from an architect's point of view, this is usually the most labour-intensive stage. However, an architect can only include what you've already decided so make sure you've worked through all the various elements together before the drawings are completed.

SPECIFICATION OF WORKS

This is a detailed explanation of all works to be priced. Unless your specification covers every part of the build, your quotes will include different interpretations of what is needed to execute the project.

Your specification should cover all aspects of the build, from demolition to finishes, and should be used in conjunction with your construction drawings. If you're having difficulty detailing how you want something done, use photos and diagrams to clarify what you mean. You should include information about the site location, access and any site-specific constraints, e.g. if there's no side passage, everything will have to be carried through the house. These details can affect costs and the builders might not request a site visit before submitting their tender.

OTHER DOCUMENTS

These usually include costing documents and a list of PC (prime cost) sums. A costing document (this is normally referred to as schedule of rates or bill of quantities, depending on your contract) allows the contractor to provide an itemised list of costs. All builders must complete and return this detailed document so that you can compare itemised quotes. It also simplifies the inevitable value engineering (cost cutting) process and you may find that once you've given up on your dreams of a mezzanine level or a landscaped garden, you have a wider choice of builders.

As well as structural elements, such as chimneys and fireplaces, all carpentry should be included in construction drawings.
Architect: DMVF | Photographer: Ruth Maria Murphy

TENDER PREPARATION

Unless you are tendering for a relatively small and specific job, e.g. new windows, it is advisable to employ the services of an architect or quantity surveyor for tender preparation. In fact, for most larger jobs, you are likely to have a number of professionals involved at this stage. An architect will advise you on whether or not you need a structural engineer. If energy efficiency is important to you, you may want to talk to an energy consultant. If a new kitchen is part of your design, you should seek the advice of a kitchen designer. While an in-house kitchen designer may draw up plans in the hope of selling you a kitchen, most consultants will need to be paid cold, hard cash. Don't skimp on this – it will be more cost effective in the end as it will ensure you get an efficient and effective design.

The first part of tender preparation is to finalise the details of your finishes, in particular the big ticket items, such as kitchen, sanitary ware, flooring and windows. This forces you to think about how each room will be used and laid out. For example, while furniture does not need to be decided on right now, if you have an idea of the size and shape of what you need, you can keep an eye out for suitable pieces. You may want to talk to an interior designer before finalising your fixtures and fittings. You should also consider hard landscaping at this stage, as there can be cost savings (such as labour and machinery) when you have your builder on site.

DON'T SKIMP ON PROFESSIONAL ADVICE – IT WILL BE MORE COST EFFECTIVE IN THE END.

Kitchen and bathroom layouts need to be decided before tender documents are finalised.
1. Architect: DMVF | Photographer: Ruth Maria Murphy
2. Architect: Broadstone | Photographer: Aisling McCoy

TENDER PROCESS

There are two common ways of tendering. The first is a negotiated tender – this is where you already have a builder that you are happy to work with. In this case, the tender process consists of negotiating prices for each job to be done. This may not result in the best price but it might be worth it to have a trusted and safe pair of hands in charge of your build.

The second (and more common) method is the competitive tender, where several contractors are given identical tender documents and asked to price all itemised jobs. It is usual to send a tender package to

four to six interested parties. An architect will have a panel of approved builders, but if you don't have one involved at this stage, ask around for recommendations of builders that have completed similar types of work. Talk to the builders, ask for references and, most importantly, visit their work. If you have any reservations, walk away.

When you're preparing your tender documents, set a return date of two to four weeks. The prices you receive back may vary wildly so make sure you go through each one line by line to see exactly what you have been

This early twentieth-century cottage has been reconfigured and extended to more than twice its original size.
Architect: Amanda Bone | Photographer: Ros Kavanagh

quoted for – it could be that one builder has priced a particular job way higher or lower than the others. If all quotes are higher than expected, don't freak out! Instead, simply sit down and work out which items you can live without or save for a later date. This process is called value engineering. En suites, utility rooms, fireplaces and landscaping commonly get set aside at this stage.

Once you have given equal consideration to all quotes, shortlist the two most favourable ones and, if necessary, ask for any clarifications or a further breakdown from each contractor.

You may also want to meet with the builders at this stage to get a feel for how your relationship might develop.

When you have chosen your builder, you should ask for evidence of all relevant insurance documents, details of their health and safety policy and record, references (bank, professional and customer) and if you haven't visited an example of their previous work, now is the time to do so. If everything is in order, you can then agree terms and sign contracts.

ARCHITECT'S TOP TIPS FOR TENDERING

1. The more decisions you make at the tender stage, the more cost control you will have as you move through the project.

2. Keep in mind that all contractors are not equal – some are quicker, some provide better finishes, some are more reliable and some are cheaper.

3. If you have a discussion or make a clarification with one tenderer, issue an update to them all.

4. When you receive a price, check that VAT is included and if so, at what rate. Ask for a breakdown, showing the VAT amount and rate.

5. Once you have your prices, get out your calculator and make sure that all items have been added together correctly. Then add the VAT and check again.

6. If completing a smaller project, such as a kitchen or bathroom renovation, check if the contractor's cost includes waste removal and hiring skips.

7. Do you need to move services? Moving gas and electricity meters or making new connections to public sewers or water mains can have significant costs. For some services, you need to deal directly with the utility/management companies, who will have their own set of costs.

8. Consider damage to landscaping as builders' vans and diggers tend to tear up lawns and other landscaped areas. Be clear at the outset about what areas a builder can access and, if damage is likely to be done to landscaping, check if rectifying it is included in the contract.

If you are doing a kitchen renovation, make sure you have accounted for the removal and disposal of your existing kitchen.
Interior Designer: Little Design House | Stylist: Marlene Wessels | Photographer: Ruth Maria Murphy

VICTORIAN GATE LODGE

WHO LIVES HERE:
Imelda Murphy, her husband
and children

LOCATION:
Garrykennedy, County
Tipperary

PROJECT:
Complete renovation and
extension

This nineteenth-century cottage was renovated and extended.
All images in case study: Architect: DMVF | Photographer: Peter O'Reilly

Front view of original house.

THE PROPERTY

In 2006, Imelda and her husband bought the old gate lodge to Garrykennedy House, when they were still living in the States.

'It was a tiny cottage with three rooms and a very bad 1950s kitchen and bathroom extension,' says Imelda. 'It was in really bad condition.'

The couple wanted to renovate and extend the lodge so they would have three bedrooms, one with an en suite, a laundry room, a main bathroom, a library, a sitting room and a new kitchen. Their architect was recommended by a friend.

'We wanted to stay faithful to the original cottage. We saved the stone wall in the library and the windows are the same as they were.'

The lodge has an interesting list of residents – Shane McGowan's family was said to have lived there at one stage and the family who were there in the 1930s still live fairly nearby.

'When our architect was working on the build, three people came to the gate and got chatting to him. They were related to the old gatekeepers – one of them was born here. The next day our architect received the most fabulous photo in the post – it was the family standing outside the lodge in the 1930s.'

THE TENDER

The tender process was difficult as Imelda and her husband were still on the other side of the Atlantic. While their architect suggested a number of builders, Imelda was determined to do her own research.

'I rang Nenagh Garda Station and was put onto one of the top fellas. I explained that we were over in America and getting some building work done and I asked him if he could recommend a builder. Right off the top of his tongue he gave me the name of a local guy.'

Imelda met the builder on one of her trips to Ireland and visited some of his work. She was impressed and admits she was rooting for him throughout the tender process.

'I was so delighted when he came in with the lowest quote. And with him and our architect on board, we really didn't have any worries.'

Original hall.

Original living room.

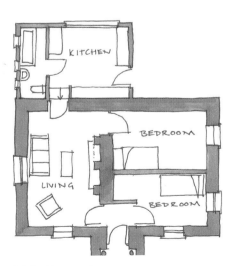

Original house plan.

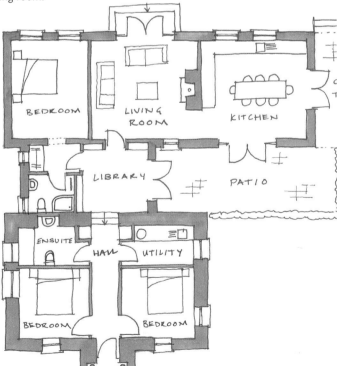

New house plan.

THE BEST BITS

Imelda loves that they were able to retain the character of the cottage, in particular the library, which has the original stone walls. She spends much of her time tending and adding to the garden, which has a stunning view of Lough Derg and sits on half an acre.

'The patio is to die for right now, it's very lush out there. I've bought new garden pots with camellias and magnolias. I've old Victorian roses and my peonies are about to burst.'

Imelda also loves her orchard, which keeps her busy.

'We get absolutely fabulous apples, an abundance every other year. This is the other year, so I'll be making the Garrykennedy chutney.'

CASE STUDY

'THE PATIO IS TO DIE FOR RIGHT NOW, IT'S VERY LUSH OUT THERE. I'VE BOUGHT NEW GARDEN POTS WITH CAMELLIAS AND MAGNOLIAS. I'VE OLD VICTORIAN ROSES AND MY PEONIES ARE ABOUT TO BURST.'

7 CONSTRUCTION

A contemporary extension has filled this nineteenth-century mews house with natural light.
Architect: DMVF | Photographer: Paul Tierney

DECISION TIME

So you've finished your drawings, got your planning permission and chosen your builder. Great stuff. You may be thinking that you've got the project this far and it's over to the professionals now. Well, yes and no. If you don't have the time or inclination to be involved in design decisions then your architect or project manager can do it all for you from now on. However, if you are managing the build yourself or you want to pick your own finishes and fixtures then you can expect to be called upon regularly to make choices. So far, all decisions may have felt somewhat abstract, in that you have had to imagine their impact on the finished product. Now, everything you choose, from lighting to flooring and windows to tiles, will be tangible and final.

The construction stage can be stressful and there may be unforeseen problems as the best laid plans can come unstuck. You won't always have time to research every last detail, and availability and lead times may limit your choices. (I could, at this stage, refer you back to Chapter 1 and the importance of preparation but I'm sure you've got this by now!) However, I'm not sure there's a more exciting and gratifying moment in the whole process than when the walls go up and you get to stand in your new space for the first time. Sure, there will be issues on site but there is no better time to sort them out than when you are face-to-face with them. Don't panic if and when this happens – it's what your contingency is for and, as design is a continuous process, sometimes a problem can provide an opportunity to improve your home. It's going to be fine and it's going to be fun.

BEFORE YOU START

Tempting as it is to get started as soon as your builder is ready, it is important to ensure that all your paperwork and responsibilities are in order first. If your bank still has to approve the final stage of your mortgage application or you're waiting for your insurance broker to confirm cover, then take a deep breath and go back to researching kitchens or whatever it is you have to do to get through the next week or two. Signed documents – contracts, insurance, financial, health and safety – will be your best friend in times of trouble so don't start the build without them.

CONTRACT

No matter how highly recommended your builders and no matter how much you love and trust them, do not dream of trying to do this without a contract. Believe it or not, a large percentage of people who spend their life savings on home renovation do so without the protection of a written contract. A standard form of contract (available from the RIAI in the Republic of Ireland and the JCT in the UK) is a tried and tested document that has evolved over time to deal with all eventualities. It is designed to be used in a project where an architect has been appointed, however it contains valuable information for anyone considering drawing up their own contract. Hopefully you won't need to refer to your contract once your build has begun but if all the eventualities are not agreed in writing, then the chance of a dispute is high. Don't take any chances – get it all nailed down in advance.

FINANCING

Make sure that you have all funds in place before you start work. You will have to make payments at specific intervals and, if a builder is not paid within the agreed timeframe, they may simply stop work and may even sue you for lost earnings. Typically, once a contractor has made a written claim for payment, your architect or QS will visit the site to value the amount of work completed and then you will be issued with a payment certificate – you usually have seven working days to pay this. If you are managing the build yourself, you need to work out payment stages and dates with your builder in advance. So, wait until all bank paperwork is signed, sealed and delivered before you begin.

If you have organised a mortgage, your bank may require a building professional to sign off on work at various stages before payments will be released. They may also need regular payment certificates, so if you don't have an architect overseeing this, you will have to arrange for a qualified building professional to complete the task.

INSURANCE

Both you and your contractor should have adequate insurance in place before you start work. Different contract types assign different insurance responsibilities – make sure both your insurances and those of your contractor match your contract obligations. For example, if you are using a RIAI standard contract, it will contain insurance clauses that will need to be complied with. You or your architect should request a copy of your builder's insurance details. It's a good idea to request that your own insurance broker clarifies in writing that your builder's insurance is adequate. No matter what size your project, you should always notify your broker about any construction and arrange the appropriate cover for your home before work commences. There are many other policies available that might apply to your project so check with your broker or insurance company and make sure that you are adequately covered.

This former bank has been transformed into a large city apartment with a roof terrace (see case study, page 169). Architect: DMVF | Photographer: Ruth Maria Murphy

+ SIGNED DOCUMENTS – CONTRACTS, INSURANCE, FINANCIAL, HEALTH AND SAFETY – WILL BE YOUR BEST FRIEND IN TIMES OF TROUBLE SO DON'T START THE BUILD WITHOUT THEM.

HEALTH AND SAFETY

You need to be aware that, as the site owner, it is your legal responsibility to ensure that your building site is safe and that your workers' health is not at risk. In the **Republic of Ireland**, for projects that have more than one contractor and that will last more than thirty days or involve a particular risk, the homeowner has specific health and safety obligations outlined by the Health and Safety Authority (see *Resources*). Two Project Supervisors must be appointed, one for the Design Process (PSDP) and one for the Construction Stage (PSCS), once you start work on site. These roles must be fulfilled by competent and qualified professionals, who will prepare and lodge the necessary paperwork on your behalf.

Similarly, in **Northern Ireland**, you must assign a Principal Designer and a Principal Contractor, if there is more than one contractor involved in your build. The Principal Designer is responsible for planning and managing health and safety in the pre-tender phase of the project and the Principal Contractor assumes this role during the construction phase. If work will last longer than 30 days and have more than 20 people working simultaneously at any point, or it exceeds 500 'person days', then you must notify the project to the Health and Safety Executive of Northern Ireland (see *Resources*).

＋ BUILDING REGULATIONS AND PLANNING PERMISSION ARE OFTEN CONFUSED AND IT IS CRUCIAL TO UNDERSTAND THAT COMPLYING WITH ONE DOES NOT OFFSET YOUR OBLIGATION TO COMPLY WITH THE OTHER.

This extension allows for a double height space in the kitchen with a mezzanine landing above.
Architect: Broadstone | Photographer: Paul Tierney

BUILDING REGULATIONS

Building regulations and planning permission are often confused and it is crucial to understand that complying with one does not offset your obligation to comply with the other. While planning officials assess a property's size, shape and materials, building regulations govern the way in which works are undertaken. These regulations are the minimum legal requirements for the design and construction of buildings, the purpose of which is to promote good practice in the interest of health, safety and welfare. In other words, they exist to ensure that your home is built properly and safely. The areas covered include structure, fire safety, ventilation, hygiene, drainage, accessibility and the conservation of fuel and power. Before starting on site, you need to make sure that you have lodged the correct documents and have received all the required paperwork from your local authority.

It is a legal requirement in both **Northern Ireland** and the **Republic of Ireland** that all new building work complies with regulations. The main difference between the two jurisdictions is that in Northern Ireland, the local authority inspects the work at set stages and issues a certificate on completion, whereas in the Republic, the homeowner is responsible for organising compliance with building regulations.

In **Northern Ireland**, if you are building a house, an extension over ten square metres, converting a roof space (attic) or you are changing the use of a building, you must make an application to the Building Control department of your local authority (see *Resources*) before you start work. Once you have received approval, you must notify Building Control of start and end dates and at specific stages of the build. On satisfactory completion of the project, they will send you a Completion Certificate, which is a required document for the sale of your home.

For any building project in the **Republic of Ireland**, the homeowner or developer has the obligation to ensure that all building works comply with the building regulations. Your obligations and the process by which you demonstrate compliance will vary depending on a number of factors including the scale, complexity and type of development. Please check your obligations with the Building Control department of your local authority and seek professional advice before undertaking any work.

Whether you are converting an attic or building a large extension, you must comply with building regulations.
Architect: DMVF | Photographer: Ruth Maria Murphy

CONSTRUCTION PROGRAMME

Residential renovations and extensions tend to follow a similar progression pattern, regardless of the amount of work you intend to do. Each tradesperson becomes involved at a particular stage so that work can be scheduled efficiently. For example, you don't want your painter showing up before your walls have been plastered or your tiler hanging around waiting for your plumber to finish. These stages can overlap to a certain extent, for example, your tiler could be tiling the upstairs bathroom floor while your plumber is fitting the boiler down-stairs.

Your builder will prepare a programme that takes all work into account, within the timeframe you have agreed. Check that your quoted lead-in times match those in the programme and if there are any products you have not yet researched, now is the time to do it. A general rule is, the higher the spec, the longer the lead-in time.

If you are project managing a number of different tradespeople yourself, then it will be up to you to schedule work appropriately. Bear in mind that the programme may change due to weather, illness, holidays or other factors, but you should try and organise jobs so that key milestones are still met.

Try not to focus too much on the finish date – the more flexible you are with this, the less stress you will endure as the project approaches completion.

✳ ARCHITECT'S TIP: Be careful of lead-in times for windows and doors. These can be long so make sure you get your order placed on time.

TYPICAL BUILD PROGRAMME

If you have an architect overseeing the build then they will guide you through the process and the decisions to be made. Your architect will inspect work at regular intervals, on average 1–2 weeks, although this will depend on the programme of the project and the scope of your agreement with your architect. If you are the boss then you will need to balance lead-in times with the relevant stages of your programme. While build programs tend to have a predictable pattern, timescales can vary hugely depending on the size and complexity of the project.

1. SITE PREPARATION

This involves the erection of hoarding for security and fencing or netting to protect adjoining properties, disconnection of utilities, demolition of existing structures, removal of trees and shrubs, and pegging out the footprint of the new structure.

Don't panic if you arrive on site and there is nobody there. Your builder's programme is theirs to organise as they see fit – maybe they've had to visit suppliers or maybe there is just nothing to do that day.

2. FOUNDATIONS

Typical foundation work includes digging out a trench to an agreed depth and laying a concrete footing. Then blockwork is built up to floor level. Concrete floors and any insulation and damp-proof or radon-proof membrane can then be put in place.

Don't be disappointed if your extension feels smaller than expected at this stage – it will look much bigger when the walls and roof go on.

3. EXTERNAL WALLS

Walls are built to first floor level using blocks or a frame. If you are having a second storey, a floor structure will be introduced and then walls will be built up to the roof. As soon as the walls go up and openings are created, you should order your windows and doors, as these usually take two to six weeks to arrive, depending on the supplier.

4. ROOFING

Residential roofs usually include a timber frame covered with slate or tiles. You may also have a flat roof covered in asphalt, metal or another material.

5. WINDOW/DOOR INSTALLATION

Windows and doors are usually fitted next to make the house watertight, but it can depend on the project. External work can then be finished.

Flooring, tiles and kitchens can have a long lead-in time (up to six weeks) and should be ordered at this stage. To be safe, you should check the lead-in times for all products. You also need to confirm all plumbing and electrical locations.

6. FIRST FIX TRADES

This refers to initial plumbing and electrical work and joinery, such as stud walls and door frames. It basically means all pipes, wires and woodwork that need to be fixed in the roof, walls and floor.

Light fittings, switches and socket plates, bathroom flooring and sanitary ware should all be ordered now. The contractor usually orders items like the boiler and radiators, architraves, stair railings and cabinetry, if they are part of the contract.

7. PLASTERING

Once first fix is finished, the walls can be insulated and plastered. This usually means a layer of plasterboard or insulated plasterboard that is skimmed on top.

Ironmongery (e.g. door handles) can be ordered now – this usually has a short lead-in time (one to two weeks).

8. SECOND FIX TRADES

Second fix is the fitting of the exposed part of the plumbing, electrical and joinery work.

- The electrician returns to put light fittings and sockets in place, appliances are fitted and everything is wired into the fuse box and meter. When the electrician is finished, they will give you a certificate to give to your electricity supplier.
- The plumber installs your boiler, radiators (rads to those in the know) and sanitary ware. Be careful here as your bathroom flooring should be installed before your WC is fitted.
- The carpenter fits your internal doors, ironmongery, skirting boards, architraves, stair railings and cabinetry.

9. FINISHES

At this stage, your home is ready for flooring, tiling, kitchen installation, fireplaces and any other finishes you have chosen.

Hard landscaping, such as paving, driveways, raised beds and water features can also be chosen and fitted now. There is not usually a long lead-in time for these items. For example, gravel is usually in stock and paving slabs take one to two weeks at the most, unless they are non-standard.

If you are nearing your completion date, don't put too much pressure on your builders as they might rush your finishes – try and find a balance between time and quality. In the meantime, your job is to spend your days and nights poring over paint charts.

You're almost there!

10. PAINTING AND DECORATING

Internal and external painting, wallpapering, oiling and varnishing complete the renovation process. All that's left for you is to add your own style and personality (see *Interiors*).

11. SNAGGING

Snagging just means getting your builder or tradesperson to finish outstanding work. It's officially referred to as 'outstanding or defect works of a trivial nature'. Don't be afraid to list everything that hasn't been finished correctly or isn't working properly.

PROJECT MANAGEMENT

The success of a building programme depends on the skills of its project manager – whether you are self-managing or employing an architect. While being able to manage time, money and quality (and deciding which comes first) is a prerequisite for the job, it's people management that really drives a trouble-free build. You will have a builder, a client, several tradespeople, professionals and suppliers, all with different personalities and requirements, and all invested in the process. The project manager needs to be able to facilitate goodwill and teamwork between all parties, particularly as these relationships can last for many months or even years.

There can be a general preconception that builders are out to make a quick buck, cutting corners and charging for hidden extras as soon as your back is turned. Building contractors are, on the whole, small business owners doing a highly technical and wide-ranging job. They also commit a huge amount of money to your project up-front and are not usually reimbursed until several weeks into the build.

The decision on whether or not to project manage yourself tends to be driven by costs. When you are faced with paying thousands to an architect, self-management may seem like an attractive option. Even if you have the expertise to oversee such a huge project, you need to consider the opportunity costs.

A renovation and new extension completely transformed this period house.
Architect: DMVF | Photographer: Paul Tierney

Rear view of original house.

Do you have the time to learn how to do the job efficiently, make contacts and then be on site every day once the build starts? Will you be saving more than you could be earning otherwise? As well as organisational skills, you need to consider whether or not you have the temperament to display authority, communicate and delegate, and remain cool under pressure. Be honest with yourself. Do you like DIY? Do you enjoy face-to-face resolution? Do you love spreadsheets?

The truth is that, even if you can answer yes to all the hard questions, you may not save much, if anything, in the end. A lack of experience in planning and coordinating a build can result in mistakes that will cause scheduling and cost overruns. If you do it yourself, you are also relying on several different tradespeople, who have no ongoing relationship with you, to turn up on time and finish on schedule. Similarly, a contractor has little hope of further work from you so may not go above and beyond their contractual obligations. If you are ordering materials yourself, you will likely miss out on economies of scale, trade discounts and the lower VAT rate charged to builders. Keep in mind also how the long hours and constant demands will affect close family and other interested parties. However, if you enjoy the thought of the challenge, the risk, the stress and the physical labour and everyone is on board with this, go for it!

THATCHED COTTAGE

WHO LIVES HERE:
Patti O'Neill (Architect)

LOCATION:
Nenagh, County Tipperary

PROJECT:
Conservation and renovation

Original house.

This eighteenth-century cottage was renovated using traditional techniques. All images in case study: Architect: Patti O'Neill | Photographers: Philip Lauterbach & Penny Crawford-Collins

THE PROPERTY

In 2013, Patti bought a 250-year-old thatched cottage with an extension that was added around 1880. She dated the building using ordnance survey maps and a draft promissory note from 1853, found inside a wall.

Patti wanted to use the proper conservation techniques to return the cottage to its original state and, in doing so, create a cosy and comfortable home.

'The floor level had been raised so many times, most likely because of a rising water table causing damp, that you couldn't walk through the doorways of the house without bending over. The walls were also covered in layers of render and concrete – all of that had to go.'

THE CONSTRUCTION

In total, over 60 tonnes of cement and concrete were removed from the walls, floor and exterior paths.

'I did a pretty hardcore job in that I got rid of all the cement,' says Patti. 'I took all the cement off the floors and I took three inches of render off the walls inside, revealing windows throughout the house.'

Outside, Patti replaced the concrete lintels with stone. Inside, she put a leca and lime mix on the floors for breathable, vapour-permeable insulation so that any dampness in the ground could dissipate naturally.

'On top of that, I put in a limecrete floor slab and in that layer, I have underfloor heating. Then I put in flint to grind it down as otherwise it doesn't harden.'

Patti also dug trenches around the house to act as an external rainwater drain.

'That had never been done before because they didn't have the machines back then – everything was done by hand.'

Inside the house, Patti left some of the walls bare and, with others, she experimented with colour pigments in whitewash.

'It gives you a sense of a hue of the colour so when light falls on it, it's very calming.'

The experience has taught Patti to use healthy, breathable materials in all her work, whether she is renovating a traditional building or designing a modern one.

Original house.

Original kitchen.

Original house plan.

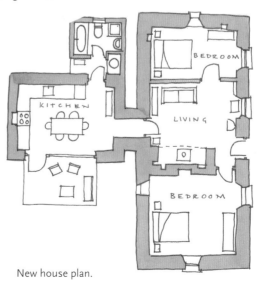

New house plan.

★ CASE STUDY

THE BEST BITS

Patti's favourite spots change, depending on the time of day. **'I love sitting on my sofa with the** fire on being able to look out the **glass door, but my favourite spot right now is sitting outside in the** sun.'

'I LOVE SITTING ON MY SOFA WITH THE FIRE ON BEING ABLE TO LOOK OUT THE GLASS DOOR, BUT MY FAVOURITE SPOT RIGHT NOW IS SITTING OUTSIDE IN THE SUN.'

8 INTERIORS

The flooring and colour schemes provide a unifying theme that links these rooms together.
Architect: DMVF | Photographer: Ruth Maria Murphy

THE FINAL LAYER

Whether you've just survived a build or are simply looking to breathe new life into your home, it's time to look at finishes and furnishings, the final aesthetic layer that brings your style and personality into your home. Getting your interiors right is not simple. It involves working with the principles of interior design, having an awareness of how each element fits into the overall plan and knowing when it's okay to break all the rules. And once you've mastered that part of it, you get to spend countless hours sourcing the perfect products.

If you have been involved to any extent in the design process so far, you won't come to this chapter unprepared. You will know all about light, colour and texture and the importance of looking at how all three elements interact with and affect each other. You will also have a collection of photos and moodboards that represent the interior styles and ambiences that you are drawn to. And if you've come straight to this section, welcome on board! Your homework is to immerse yourself in Houzz, Pinterest, interiors websites and blogs, and to go and have a read of Chapter 2: *Design*.

This chapter is about how you create layers of interest in your new space, within an overall scheme of unity and harmony. What that means is that each room should have its own look and feel while also complementing the other rooms to strengthen the composition of the home as a whole.

Of course, taste is in the eye of the beholder and is dependent on culture, fashion and personal experience: one person's elegant is another person's boring. Trends and preferences change over time, now more quickly than ever, thanks to how easy it is to access images. While the last couple of decades saw a move towards minimalism, current trends incorporate lush, intimate, dark and dramatic styles – clutter is cool again!

So when it comes to your interiors, don't just ask yourself, 'do I love it?', but instead: 'Will I love it in five years' time?' Not such a biggie for wall colours or even tiles but when you're buying a kitchen, hardwood flooring or a sofa, you want it to stand the test of time. As long as you get the fundamentals right, you can have a bit of fun experimenting with the more transient, less expensive design elements.

Interior Designer: On The Square Emporium, Belfast | Stylist: Marlene Wessels | Photographer: Ruth Maria Murphy

FINDING YOUR STYLE

If you've spent months or years poring over photos of interiors or glued to home renovation programmes, then you may well come to the project with a fully-formed vision for your home. For many people, the specifics of interior design are not really on their radar until it's time to focus on their own home. Much as I love fashion and design, I never noticed other people's light fittings or kitchen cabinets before I started sourcing my own. However, thanks to a long planning process, I had plenty of time to investigate different styles and eras and to think about colour schemes and textures. I tried to visualise the relationship between space, furniture and accessories, and light and colour. In the long months waiting for planning decisions, I used to spend evenings in our empty shell of a house, walking around the interior and exterior space with a measuring tape in my hand and my imagination on zoom. I'm not sure if our interiors would have come together so quickly and cohesively had I not developed such an intimate relationship with the original house. Of course, we had never lived in it, so if you have spent several years in your home, you will already have a connection with it, although it may be one that needs a bit of distance or intervention to redefine itself.

It is crucial to match your interiors to your architecture so make sure to keep this in mind throughout the project. Images you've pulled out of magazines, your Houzz and Pinterest photos and any other moodboards you have prepared will be invaluable at this stage. Your architect will use them to interpret your style and to help you develop your interiors accordingly. If you don't have a professional involved then bring your photos to kitchen, furniture, flooring and decorating showrooms and let the salespeople there help you recreate the looks you like. If you are unsure of how to begin, it could be worth having a consultation with an interior designer to develop an overall plan. A few hundred euro/pounds' worth of advice at this stage could make all the difference to the final product.

✱ **ARCHITECT'S TIP:** Form should always follow function. What that means is that the function of an object comes first and the form or shape is based on that functionality. For example, a kitchen should serve all your needs, and once those are decided, you can look at shape and materials.

THE FIVE PRINCIPLES OF INTERIOR DESIGN

In Chapter 2, we looked at the elements of architectural design in terms of people, place and space, and focused on how light, colour and texture all work together to create a visual and emotional presence. Now we're going to focus on the principles of interior design, which help to give a coherent structure to all the elements of a room and, in turn, a home. Keep in mind the intersection of light, colour and texture while you consider each principle and try to visualise your rooms in this context.

1. UNITY

Your home should follow a unifying theme that gives the sense that all of the parts are working together to create a common result. That doesn't mean that all your rooms need to have the same style or even to follow the same era, but there does need to be a common thread that runs throughout your home. Without it, you will have visual interruptions as you move or look from one area to another. The easiest way to create a harmonising flow is with colour. Rather than choosing the colour of each space in isolation, make sure that it blends and flows as you move from one room to the next. For example, a blue/grey/green theme gives scope for using dramatic yet complementary colours throughout the home. Finishes such as flooring or wall panelling can do a great job of linking spaces, while the repetition of textiles and patterns can create rhythm (see page 156) across spaces.

The same principle of unity applies within each space, with colour, texture and form providing a compositional framework. You can also create unity in contrast if similar variations occur in linked spaces. For example, light coloured furniture against dark flooring across two rooms creates unity between the rooms, if not necessarily within them.

2. SCALE AND PROPORTION

The principles of scale and proportion ensure that objects placed in a space look like they belong there. For example, a high-ceilinged room needs to have tall furniture, and a big sofa looks better with large, plump cushions. When you put a piece of furniture in a room and it just doesn't feel right, the most likely culprit is scale or proportion. Scale refers to the size of elements within a space and in relation to our own human form, whereas proportion generally relates to the ratio of one object to another. Scale tends to be absolute in that it can be measured and there are standardised heights for some design elements, such as countertops and chairs. Proportion is largely in the eye of the beholder and, for example, an oversized light pendant that works in one room may not have the same effect in another.

SCALE REFERS TO THE SIZE OF ELEMENTS WITHIN A SPACE AND IN RELATION TO OUR OWN HUMAN FORM, WHEREAS PROPORTION GENERALLY RELATES TO THE RATIO OF ONE OBJECT TO ANOTHER.

An object that fills two-thirds of the available space gives the best sense of proportion.
Architect: DMVF | Photographer: Ruth Maria Murphy

If you are looking for a general rule for scale and proportion, the Golden Ratio is a good place to start. It's a mathematical sequence, closely related to the Fibonacci Sequence, that has been found to occur over and over again in nature, art, architecture and music. There's something within us that finds this ratio (1:1.618 to be precise) pleasing and comfortable.

To put it simply, an object that fills 1:1.618 or two-thirds of the available space will give the best sense of proportion. So, buy a sofa that is two-thirds the width of the area it will occupy or a piece of artwork that runs two-thirds of the way across your mantelpiece. Similarly, a kitchen island that is two-thirds as wide as the rest of the kitchen will look perfectly in proportion.

3. BALANCE

The principle of balance refers to the way in which items of equal visual weight are arranged to create equilibrium in a room. Balance can be symmetrical, asymmetrical or radial.

SYMMETRICAL BALANCE

You can achieve this type of balance when a space is divided into two equal halves, which are centred around an axis. This axis can be a physical object, such as a fireplace or a coffee table, or it can be an imaginary line around which similar objects are organised. A pair of candlesticks placed at either end of a mantelpiece or two identical armchairs or sofas on opposite sides of a coffee table are examples of symmetrical balance. While a mainstay of traditional interiors, this style can feel quite formal in a contemporary setting and, due to its rigidity, can be difficult to achieve without compromise.

ASYMMETRICAL BALANCE

By using dissimilar elements that have equal visual weight, you can create a more relaxed feel. For example, armchairs of a similar size and scale but a different shape and colour or texture feel more casual and less contrived, and using two or more objects to balance with another of similar overall proportions creates more interest in a room. Asymmetry gives the impression of movement and results in more lively interiors.

RADIAL BALANCE

Radial balance involves a central focal point, such as a chandelier or a dining table, from which all other elements of the room radiate. It is not the most typical of room arrangements, although it can provide an interesting convergence if you use it effectively.

4. FOCAL POINT

Without areas of interest to draw the eye, your space risks becoming boring. Every room should have at least one point of emphasis, around which other elements are organised. The most common of these are fireplaces and TVs (although a TV can become dominant by default, which can cause its own issues). If you don't have a natural focal point in a room, you can create one around a work of art or a piece of furniture. It must be strong enough to draw attention and interesting enough to encourage the viewer to look further. A bold colour or pattern can draw the eye towards a corner or alcove, where accessories or furniture or both can offer an intriguing nook. Don't forget to maintain balance so the focal point does not overpower the rest of the room.

1. Symmetrical balance is used in more traditional interiors. Designer: Maven | Photographer: Bradley Quinn
2. A piece of art can create a focal point in a room. Architect/Interior Designer: Optimise Design | Stylist: Ciara O'Halloran | Artist: Andrea Flanagan | Photographer: Ruth Maria Murphy
3. Radial balance gives a central point of interest to a room. Architect: DMVF | Photographer: Derek Robinson
4. Asymmetrical balance gives a casual, relaxed feel to a room. Architect/Interior Designer: Optimise Design | Photographer: Ruth Maria Murphy

5. RHYTHM

Just as in music, design can have identifiable beats and patterns. The principle of rhythm in interior design suggests a connected movement between objects that may have a different visual weight, colour or texture. When a single characteristic, such as colour, is repeated, the spaces between the objects create a sense of rhythm. This can be achieved by repetition, progression, contrast or transition.

- Repetition is the use of the same property more than once – you can repeat colour, pattern, texture or any other element.

- Progression involves taking an element and then repeating it, using an increasing or decreasing amount of one of its properties. A cluster of candles of different sizes or cushions in various hues of the same colour are examples of progression. Generally, if you pair objects in odd numbers, they are more visually appealing and memorable than those in even-numbered pairings. This ties in with the Golden Ratio and the more relaxed and natural feel of asymmetric balance.

- Contrast is simply putting two opposing elements together, such as black and white cushions on a sofa, or round and square picture frames together on a wall. This approach provides areas of interest that draw the eye, but it can also be quite jarring so it is best if you use it sparingly.

- Transition is created by allowing the eye to move smoothly from one area or room to another. This can be achieved by the use of a continuous line in the form of shelving or coving, or by using an architectural feature such as an archway. Transition is especially important in open-plan rooms with different zones – you should make sure that each area has elements of unity that allow a smooth transition to the others.

1. The repetition of similar patterns on the chair, cushion and plant pot gives a rhythm to the room. 2. The progression of the Russian dolls gives a sense of movement to the fireplace. | Architect: DMVF | Photographer: Ruth Maria Murphy

PRACTICAL CONSIDERATIONS

Before you spend any money on that eight-seater dining table or that super king size bed, make sure that access will not be an issue. Measure everything. I can't stress this enough. You need to size up your door openings, your side entrance and the floor to ceiling heights on your stairs. Keep a measuring tape permanently in your pocket and note the height, width and depth of all furniture you view. If you are buying online, make sure you have all the stats before you purchase. Think also about access through the home – if a sofa or a piano gets through the front door, will it have room to turn corners to get into the required space?

If you've set your heart on a piece of furniture (or you own it already) and you can tell that it won't fit through the door or up the stairs, think about bringing it on site before doors, windows or stairs are installed. We had to get our super king size mattress to the first floor before the staircase went in or it would have got stuck between the fourth step and the landing overhead.

Assume nothing. While there are standard widths for kitchen units and heights for countertops, there is no absolute rule. And did you know that there are two different counter heights and bar stools to match? This would explain why the bar stools didn't fit under the counter in a rental I once lived in.

When you're taking measurements, don't forget about skirting, architraves, picture rails, coving, radiators and light fittings. This is especially important when fitting wardrobes, bookcases or other built-in units. Make sure also that there is enough room to open the doors of fitted furniture. Similarly, if you are fitting attic stairs, ensure the ladder can open fully into the floor space below.

The kitchen has become a social space as well as a functional one.
Architect: DMVF | Photographer: Paul Tierney

ROOM BY ROOM

KITCHEN/DINING

For many people, the kitchen is the most important room in the house, the heart of the home. The rise in popularity of combined cooking/eating/living spaces has led to the demise of the formal dining room and many home renovations begin by converting this room into a more usable space. It's not just a trend towards a more relaxed way of dining. The whole process of preparing food, eating it and cleaning up after it has become more social, as we spend more time together (even when we are engaged in our own virtual worlds).

More than with any other room, it is essential to get the specifications of your kitchen right. It needs to be functional, hard-wearing, easy to clean, easy to access, calming, inspiring and comfortable, and it needs storage, storage and more storage. No pressure then!

You may have heard of the kitchen 'work triangle'. This is a traditional ergonomic concept that connects three key working areas in the kitchen – the sink, the fridge and the cooker, the idea being that they form a triangle for ease of access. I find it more useful to make a triangle of the food preparation/chopping area and the sink and cooker. This works well if you have a stand alone island unit or a peninsula (a unit that is attached to the wall), especially if it means you can chat to people opposite you while you work. Have a think about how you move around your current kitchen, what works for you and what doesn't.

Another ergonomic concern is the height of your oven(s). An oven that is integrated at eye-level, as opposed to a free-standing or range oven, means that you don't have to bend down to put food in or to take it out. Similarly, having a raised dishwasher may be more comfortable and efficient. However, aesthetics also play a part and it's up to you to decide on priorities. Do make sure that all crockery, glassware and cutlery storage is within easy reach of your dishwasher and that all doors and drawers can open simultaneously. It's also handy to place bins and a dishwasher on either side of your sink.

When choosing materials for your kitchen, make sure they are durable and will withstand heat, water, spillages, droppages, children, pets and red wine. That fruit-forward pinot noir you picture yourself sipping triumphantly in your new kitchen could become your nemesis if you're not careful. Marble makes a beautiful worktop but it's a porous natural stone and it absorbs liquids. An oiled oak floor may be the perfect partner to your gloss cupboards but just watch that oily pesto seep into the grain. Ask suppliers for samples of flooring, worktops and cupboard doors, take them home and do your worst – stab them, scrape them, leave hot cups of coffee on them, drop heavy objects on them, soak them in red wine, water and olive oil. Rigorous testing is the only way to know for sure if a material can survive your lifestyle.

✱ ARCHITECT'S TIP: A kitchen island is not just a trend. Traditionally, the sink and adjoining worktop was the hub of the kitchen, and was located in front of the single window to the rear garden. Now that most people have a dishwasher and kitchens have a greater connection with the outdoors, there are other options for meal preparation.

An island unit allows the user to work at a counter while chatting to friends or family across the room or perhaps they are enjoying a glass of wine or a cup of coffee at the other end of the island. It also facilitates a view of the garden and if there are small children around, it's an easy way to keep an eye on them while preparing lunch or dinner. Many clients locate the sink or the hob on the island too, which may disturb the clean lines but can be worth it in terms of practicality.

DO MAKE SURE THAT ALL CROCKERY, GLASSWARE AND CUTLERY STORAGE IS WITHIN EASY REACH OF YOUR DISHWASHER AND THAT ALL DOORS AND DRAWERS CAN OPEN SIMULTANEOUSLY. IT'S ALSO HANDY TO PLACE BINS AND A DISHWASHER ON EITHER SIDE OF YOUR SINK.

Easy to access, clever storage can make the most of your kitchen.
Architect: DMVF | Photographer: Ruth Maria Murphy

A pendant light and strong colours can mark out the dining area in a room.
Designer: Maven | Photographer: Sarah Fyffe

DESIGNER'S TOP TIPS FOR KITCHEN LAYOUT

1. Make sure you get the best use of space possible in terms of storage and functionality.

2. Think about appliances, pull-out storage, lighting and whether the wall units should have regular or lift-up hinges.

3. Don't focus too much on finishes at the start – get the layout right and you can decide on the finish later on.

4. The most useful storage features are pull-out drawers for larders or base units, drawers with hidden cutlery trays and corner pull-out mechanisms.

Melanie Flood, Kitchen Designer, Eco Interiors

While a separate dining room is no longer a feature of many homes, a dining zone in an open-plan room has become a staple of modern renovations. However, so much planning and design goes into the kitchen and living sections of the room that there is a danger that the dining area can become neglected and end up simply as a place in which to put a table and chairs. The best way to avoid this is to define the space with a large pendant light that hangs over the table. The use of colour and pattern can also bring a visual coherence to the area – wallpaper or artwork in an alcove or a large rug can help to mark out the dining area as a distinct space.

While a dining table is a largely functional purchase and should be built to last, don't be afraid to make some bold choices when it comes to chairs. Steer clear of the once-ubiquitous brown leather dining chairs and choose colour and texture. Mix and match different styles and materials and bring some vibrancy to meal time.

The use of colour, rugs and artwork can help define a dining area in an open-plan room.
Architect: Amanda Bone | Photographer: Ros Kavanagh

LIVING

You can really have some fun with your living room. Throw out the rule book and throw yourself into this room. Don't hold back, don't play safe – experiment with colour and texture. The worst that can happen is that you need to buy some more paint. Your room's general layout may be dictated by windows, doors and fireplaces but, if possible, don't push your furniture right up against the walls – it is much more intimate to have a chair close to a sofa or the fire.

Lighting is what will make this room cosy and interesting. Overhead lighting is not necessary in a living room but if you do have it, make sure it has company as it can be unflattering on its own and it doesn't usually create the sort of atmosphere that is conducive to relaxing, entertaining and chatting. Use as many lamps as your corners and alcoves can take – seven or eight light sources of varying sizes and luminescence will create layers of intrigue and interest. Make sure you plan for enough sockets and light switches or dimmers in your tender drawings.

Colour is the variable that will make the biggest difference to your living room. It's also the easiest thing to fix if it all goes horribly wrong. Don't be afraid of dark colours as a rich colour can be a great way to create a cosy and warm room. So, go for a little luxury and try a rich, dark blue or a plush, deep maroon. Your head is probably saying grey but your heart will thank you for the depth and style of a dark hue. And if your heart really is set on grey walls then contrast with a yellow armchair or a turquoise sofa. Fabrics and artwork can introduce strong pops of colour and texture that will draw the eye to all corners of the room.

Dark, rich colours are a great way to create a cosy room.
Interior Designer: Dust Design | Photographer: Ruth Maria Murphy

Use as many layers as you can – footstools, side tables, window seats and pouffes all create areas of appeal as well as functionality. A number of small side tables can provide more interest than one larger coffee table and allow for a greater variation of room layouts. Make sure that everything is not the same height – if all your seating is at a similar level, add higher tables or plants for balance and don't be afraid to use all the available space.

If your living room is part of an open-plan room then you need to consider both how it defines itself and how it unifies with the rest of the space. A modular, L-shaped sofa can help enclose the living space. Think about the transition from this area to your kitchen and/or dining area. If you want to use strong, lush colours here, but brighter neutrals in your kitchen and dining zones, then choose complementary shades. A dark feature wall or alcove may also help to anchor your living space. Repetition of colour, pattern or artwork throughout a large space can bring unity and harmony to distinctly separate zones.

Accessories of differing heights will provide layers of interest in a room.
Designer: Maven | Photographer: Sarah Fyffe

BEDROOM

Bedrooms can suffer from blandness as most of us don't spend money on much more than the basics. However, put a little time and effort into lighting and texture and your bedroom can become somewhere you want to sneak off to.

As with your living room, plenty of subtle lighting will make your bedroom a calm and atmospheric place. At the design stage, make sure you plan for enough light and socket switches at your bedside. Also, if you are the sort of person (cough) who brings your devices to bed, make sure you have enough sockets or USB ports nearby. Of course, you absolutely shouldn't do this. For proper zen relaxation, leave your phone and tablet at a charging station downstairs.

Textures can make all the difference in a bedroom. Cotton and linen sheets are soft without being stifling, while heavy velvet curtains or throws can add layers of luxury. But the best thing you can do for your bedroom is to treat your feet – rugs, all shapes, sizes and softness. The single biggest improvement to my bedroom is a small sheepskin rug on the floor beside the bed. Every time I get in or out of bed, I pause for a moment to enjoy the sheer delight of it. Even waking in the night for the loo (three kids) loses its irritation when I remember the rug, that's how good it is.

Children's bedrooms are usually last on the renovation list, with hand-me-down beds and wardrobes acting as indefinite placeholders. However, all it takes is a few small details to transform your child's bedroom from drab to dramatic. Try a bright, fresh blue, green, yellow or pink on the walls and some bedding to match or contrast. Again, lighting can set the mood and the theme. Wall decals or stickers are an easy way of changing the space from plain to themed. Similarly, fairy lights and artwork can transform the look and feel of the room. A lick of paint is a simple facelift for a tired pine bedframe or wardrobe. If space is an issue, think about a loft bed with a desk and drawers underneath – keep an eye on second-hand websites as this is something that is generally used for a limited time and then sold on.

There's really no need to spend huge amounts of money on your five- or six-year-old's bedroom, especially as you can be guaranteed he won't appreciate the Darth Vader paraphernalia when he's twelve (but don't throw it out – he'll treasure it when he's forty!).

Subtle lighting will bring calm to your bedroom. | A few small details can transform a child's bedroom.
Designer: Maven | Photographer: Sarah Fyffe

BATHROOM

The bathroom is one place where a small amount of investment can go a long way. Functionality is the key priority here, but just because you may be limited in size and scope, it doesn't mean you can't make it a joyous place to be. For example, a vintage vanity unit or an old washstand can give your room the character it needs to avoid looking like a hotel bathroom, and clever placement of lighting and colour will take the clinical edge off hard surfaces. Rich coloured walls with accent lighting over pictures or photos can create pockets of interest and set a cosy and relaxed mood.

Bathroom layout needs to be included in tender documents so you need to plan it from the start. If you are replumbing your home, you have more options in terms of changing the layout of the bathroom and the position of the room itself within the house. Keep in mind that it will need to be close to the soil vent pipe, which carries the waste and drainage to the main sewage system. If you have a number of plumbing upgrades planned, it is a good idea to get them all done at the same time due to the disruption they will cause. Economies of scale mean it will also cost less.

If space is limited (as it usually is in a bathroom, especially an en suite), a wet room is a great way of incorporating a shower, especially into an awkward corner or alcove. A glass screen can help contain water and serve as a way of delineating the shower from the rest of the room. While bathroom storage is important, you may be surprised at how little you need once you've thrown out all those bottles you haven't used in three years. Recessed shelving and ledges can provide surfaces for most regularly-used items without encroaching on your room, while vanity units make the most of the space under your basin.

You may think that a downstairs loo leaves little scope for creativity but this could not be further from the truth! It is the one room where no design decision is out of bounds. That loud, patterned wallpaper you loved that you couldn't commit to using in your living room alcoves – bring it on; the risqué painting you thought was too much for the hall – this is its natural home. The tiny downstairs bathroom should always contain something to make you smile. And don't forget, it is the one room that visitors are guaranteed to see so make it interesting – family snaps and portraits are the perfect distraction for a guest with a couple of minutes to kill.

Subtle lighting and clever storage can make the most of your bathroom.
Interior Architecture: Maria Fenlon | Photographer: Gareth Byrne

ARCHITECT'S TIPS FOR BATHROOM DESIGN

1. Consider painting part of your bathroom rather than tiling everywhere. This will add colour and texture as well as saving you money, and you can update the room easily in the future with a lick of paint.

2. It is generally a good idea to provide both a regular and a towel radiator.

3. Don't forget to provide a place for everything that needs to be stored there – toilet rolls, cleaning equipment, cosmetics and towels.

4. Consider using underfloor heating – a delightful treat for keeping toes warm in winter.

5. Use a heat-pad on your mirror to stop it from fogging up with steam.

6. Spend money on a good quality power shower.

7. Wall-hung toilets and basins are easier to clean and make the space look bigger.

8. Provide large mirrors. Relatively speaking, these are not expensive and add light and depth to any room.

9. Don't be afraid to use colour – dark colours can make your bathroom feel luxurious and rich, while vibrant and bright colours are great for children's and family bathrooms.

10. Consider ageing and lifelong living when planning bathrooms. Having a larger downstairs loo and possibly a shower may become invaluable for you or a family member in the future.

11. If you don't have scope for a large window, consider adding a roof light to an upstairs bathroom – this can flood the room with natural light.

OFFICE

If, like me, you work from home then a self-contained office is a must. Good Wi-Fi, plenty of sockets and an adjustable-height chair and desk is all I ask. If the room is too interesting, then other people want to spend time there and this is not something I want to encourage! I do sit beside a window and that is all the distraction I need.

However, most people are more interested in fitting a work station into an existing room and this is usually easy to accommodate, especially in an open-plan room. Alcoves and corners are great places in which to nestle a printing and filing station, with enough desk space for a laptop. A larger space can also double as a homework area. If your Wi-Fi router is not close to your work space, invest in some good boosters to ensure the signal reaches all areas of your home.

UTILITY ROOM

As utility rooms are usually small, it's important to make the best use of the available space. Think about stacking your washing machine and dryer on top of each other and plan for at least one tall unit in which you can hide away brooms and mops.

An overhead rack on a pulley will provide a large drying area for laundry of all sizes and is one of the most useful gadgets to have in any home. A drying cupboard, in which you can hang your wet clothes, is another useful addition – this should be vented and can also be heated.

Good natural and mechanical ventilation is a must, especially as utility rooms are usually placed in dark and windowless parts of the home.

ALCOVES AND CORNERS ARE
GREAT PLACES IN WHICH
TO NESTLE A PRINTING
AND FILING STATION, WITH
ENOUGH DESK SPACE FOR A
LAPTOP.

1. An overhead rack on a pulley is a great space-
saving device. | Designer: Newcastle Design
2. A home office or homework space can be
integrated into a larger room. | Architect: Bright
Designs | Photographer: Kevin Woods
3. Stacking your washing machine and dryer on top
of each other can save space. | Architect: DMVF |
Photographer: Ruth Maria Murphy

CLOAKROOM/MUDROOM

Every home should have a cloakroom, whether it's simply a cupboard or a separate room. The amount of clutter generated by the things we discard when we enter the house is immense and being able to close the door on coats, shoes, bags, hats, scarves and umbrellas should be a priority. When you add kids and school and sports bags to the mix, it becomes a necessity. Whatever the size of your cloakroom, try to allocate a locker, shelf or hook for each child to store coats, shoes and bags – knowing where each of those items are every morning will save your sanity. Getting your kids to use these spaces themselves, well, you're on your own there. If you find a failsafe method, do drop me a line.

PLAYROOM

The most important thing to remember when designing a playroom is that it won't be a playroom for long. Plan for it to be a functioning living room, office or bedroom in a few years' time. Make use of flexible, modular storage rather than built-in units or obviously child-oriented furniture. Rugs and pictures can

brighten up the room and make it an inspiring place for your little ones, and can also be easily removed when they're not so little any more.

Colourful rugs and accessories can help turn an office or a bedroom into a playroom.
Architect: DMVF | Photographer: Paul Tierney

TOP TIPS FOR SOURCING FURNISHINGS

1. Buy only what you need and make sure you love it. If you love it but you can't afford it, save up and get it later – you don't have to buy everything at once.

2. Buy second hand and online. Haggle.

3. Try and stay away from mass-produced furniture.

4. Do obsess over the perfect sideboard, cocktail chair and paint colour. But if you find yourself drowning in choice, just make

a decision and move on – the end result does not hinge on every tiny detail.

5. Don't forget your budget.

6. Take a step back at times to see the difference between what you really need and what you think you need. Just because Houzz has done a feature on fancy kitchen taps, this does not mean that you need to spend €400 on a tap. I've a friend who did that and the, ahem, friend is still thinking the money could have been better spent elsewhere.

GEORGIAN APARTMENT

WHO LIVES HERE:
Colm Doyle and his partner,
Peter O'Reilly

LOCATION:
Camden Street, Dublin 2

PROJECT:
Change of use, complete
renovation, roof garden

This renovation saw two deserted Georgian buildings converted into a large city apartment.
Architect: DMVF | Photographer: Ruth Maria Murphy

Rear of original house.

THE PROPERTY

In 2014, Colm and Peter bought a disused
bank in the centre of Dublin. Spread across
two Georgian houses, the property had been
unoccupied for nearly a decade.

'I always wanted to live in a large apartment
with a good size balcony,' says Colm, 'and
I wanted to live in the city. So, I found this
building that was unloved and vacant, in very
poor condition and nobody else wanted it. We
bought a lot of building for very little money
and spent quite a lot renovating it.'

'We don't have good apartment stock in Dublin,
which is unusual for a city of its size. Most of it
dates from the early '90s onwards.'
Colm could see the potential straight away.
'There was a big flat roof extension at the back
that I knew I could turn into a roof garden, and
there were four interconnecting rooms at first
floor level that we could make a reception floor
out of. They were the two things I spotted that
are not usually available in the city.'

There were risks involved – the couple needed to get planning permission to change the use of the building and for the roof garden.

'There is not much case law or legislation around apartments in older buildings in Ireland compared to the UK. Everybody lives in houses here, there just hasn't been much of an appetite for it.'

With planning secured, Colm's brief was to create a home for himself and Peter in the two upper floors of the Georgian building, and to make it work for modern living. With no extension planned, the design of the interior space was crucial.

'It was really important to us to have bigger rooms but also smaller rooms that were cosier

and warmer. We have zoned heating so we can heat different spaces at different times.'**

They discussed splitting the space into two duplex-style units but in the end decided to keep it as one large apartment.

'It is bigger than we wanted but we liked the four interconnecting rooms on the reception level – it's really special.'

The build itself went smoothly, thanks to Colm's experience as a project manager.

'There were no cross words, I know what to expect. We aggressively managed our budget and shopped very hard for everything. We delivered within budget but were way over time but that suited us. We didn't put anyone under any pressure.'

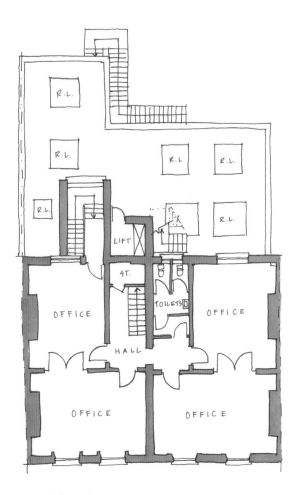

Original floor plan.

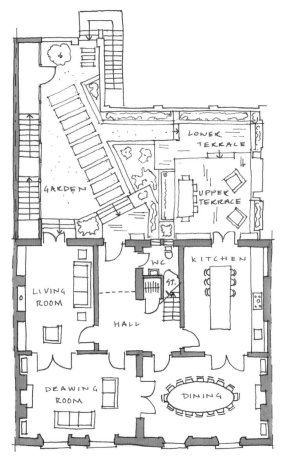

New floor plan.

Two of the original interconnecting rooms on the reception level.

THE INTERIORS

Colm retained as many original features as he could and has left the size and shape of the rooms largely unchanged.

'I wanted to retain the joy that the building had. In the more traditional rooms, I wanted to keep the floors, joinery, windows, cornicing. And we've kept the volumes of the rooms. We didn't want to carve up the spaces.'

However, he wanted all new features to stand on their own.

'The kitchen, the stove, the staircase, the bathrooms, the steel windows – we wanted them to appear as interventions. The nice thing about doing this is that it gives you some freedom.'

This freedom allowed Colm to mix and match furniture and accessories to achieve a particular feel for each room.

'I thought about what the rooms were for and what time of day I would use them and then tried to build a style around that. I wanted the kitchen to have a daytime feel and the TV room to have a cosier evening feel.'

Colm stresses that great interior design does not have to cost a huge amount of money.

'Two fireplaces came out of a skip and I painted them up. They're 1930s in an 1815 house.'

He also recommends mixing brown, traditional furniture with fun fabric choices to create a style that looks way more expensive than it is.

'Each of my dining chairs was individually cheaper than an Ikea chair and none of the chairs match.'

THE BEST BITS

Colm and Peter love the contrast between the kitchen and the TV room.

'The kitchen is bright and airy and the TV room is rich, dark and cosy.'

They also adore the roof garden and use it all the time.

Images 1 and 6 Photographer: Derek Robinson

Images 2, 3, 4, 5 Photographer: Ruth Maria Murphy

'EACH OF MY DINING CHAIRS WAS
INDIVIDUALLY CHEAPER THAN AN
IKEA CHAIR AND NONE OF THE
CHAIRS MATCH.'

9 OUTDOORS

Outdoor seating, lighting and fireplaces allow the garden to be used as a room in its own right.
Architect: DMVF | Photographer: Ros Kavanagh

A ROOM WITH A VIEW

'Bringing the outside in' is a phrase that is now commonplace in home renovation. No longer content with a single window onto the garden, most homeowners focus on opening up the back of the house to the light, warmth and view outside. This is a symbiotic relationship that also gives greater and easier access to the garden, making it an extension of the house and, potentially, a room in its own right. Outdoor seating, lighting, fireplaces, BBQs, pizza ovens and canopies have all turned the once mucky Irish garden into a habitable space that can be used for at least six months of the year. This does bring with it, however, the further challenge of landscape design – just when you thought you were finished looking at drawings and costings . . .

The good news is that if you've been paying attention so far, you're probably already halfway towards designing your garden. The design elements of light, colour and texture, and the principles of unity, scale and proportion, balance, focal point and rhythm are just as applicable to the outside of your home as the inside. And if your garden is visually accessible from indoors then it should respond to your interior design and vice versa. You can mirror the shape of your open-plan room outdoors or continue the unifying theme using the same colour or materials. If you need a refresher on any of these concepts, you'll find them in the *Design* and *Interiors* chapters.

Ultimately, what you want from your garden will drive the design and shape of it – as always, form follows function. Whether you're planning a swimming pool or a trampoline, an outdoor kitchen or a cosy corner, you'll need to prioritise your needs. However, more than a kitchen or a living room, a garden is a living, breathing system that grows and changes over time, so try not to be too prescriptive at the start. Allow your garden, and your relationship with it, the space to develop and find its own way.

GETTING STARTED

Our previous house had the teeniest yard you ever saw, with barely enough room for bins and bikes. Although I had grown up in a very hands-on gardening household, it had been several decades since I'd had the pleasure or the responsibility of a garden. But when we moved to our new house, I became the proud owner of a large pile of muck. If you've had extensive work done at the back of your house, this is what you too will be looking at from your beautifully-glazed kitchen. Do you have kids and/or pets? Good for you – this is going to be fun.

If possible, get your hard landscaping (which includes paving, decking, fencing, steps and water features) done before you move in. Having a patio or a path means that you will be able to use your outdoor space without wading through mud and dirt. However, paving is often the first thing to be cut in the value engineering, cost-cutting process so you may well need to come up with some creative solutions while you settle into your new home. If possible, get a lawn planted, even if you plan to pave over it eventually.

We had an area to the side and rear of our house paved before the builders left. Thanks to our large dog and three kids, leaving the rest of the garden au naturel was simply not an option. As it was winter, we needed to buy some time until the spring growing season so we covered the muck in weed membrane and secured it at the edges with leftover concrete blocks and paving slabs. In April, we sprayed weed killer, rotavated, raked, spread topsoil and planted grass seed. We used the weed membrane to make a fence to keep dogs and kids off the area until the grass had established. The fence wasn't fool proof so it was a long six weeks.

An alternative to this waiting game is to use roll-out turf grass as it will give you an instant lawn. However, it is significantly more expensive. You should not walk on this until the roots have knitted into the soil below, which can take up to three weeks. This was the deciding factor for us – if we were going to have to keep everyone off the grass for three weeks, we might as well tough it out for another few weeks and save ourselves a good chunk of money. Once you have a more level playing field, you can start to make plans and decide on your budget.

The first step in designing our garden was to grow a lawn, which made a great football pitch.

A traditional, rural house can lend itself to a wild and natural garden.
Architect: Patti O'Neill | Photographer: Philip Lauterbach & Penny Crawford-Collins

Extensive planting can be expensive but it is something you can do gradually in your own time.
Architect: David Flynn | Photographer: Barbara Corsico

Hard landscaping, such as paving, raised beds and water features, can transform a small garden.
Designer: Russell Shekleton, KHS Landscaping

COSTS

The bad news is that gardens cost. If you start off your landscaping project with the mindset, 'But how much can a terrace and some plants cost?' then it will take a while for the answer, 'A lot', to sink in. The good news is that, with some advice and guidance, you can do a large part of it yourself. It is advisable to have hard landscaping done by a professional, but lawns, planting and many other features can be added in your own time. And if your plan includes a shed, a trampoline or a swing set, you can leave space for this and buy it whenever finances allow.

A significant cost can be paving or decking. The materials can vary considerably in price so research different types and suppliers and shop around. Gravel can be a great substitute for both at a fraction of the cost. Consider a stepping stone path rather than a fully paved one – stone or concrete remnants and scraps can make a beautiful walkway, and if you can find enough pieces, they can also be used for a patio area.

If you want to level a sloped garden, there can be sizeable excavation costs depending on the area, the access, the soil quality and so on. To avoid having to level the entire area, one option is to put in steps at a third or two-thirds (stick to the Golden Ratio!) of the way along the garden. This will have the added bonus of creating layers of interest in your garden.

The cost of clearing your garden of old structures, unwanted materials and poor soil can come as a shock if it is not factored into your budget. Try to do this yourself in advance to save money. Think about what you can reuse and recycle and get a skip for everything else. Consider also digging out holes yourself for flower beds or an in-ground trampoline.

And remember, you don't need to do everything at once. Plan your design so that paving, paths and walls can be done in year one, planting in year two and then water features, sheds and larger shrubs or trees can be acquired whenever your budget allows.

If you are using a landscape designer then they will measure your garden and work with you to come up with a scheme. Sound familiar? Even if you are doing or managing all the work yourself, it's worth having a consultation with a professional. Having an expert look critically at your space and suggest a layout, with suitable materials and plants, will get you started in the right direction.

When you are working out your budget, don't forget about all the things that will need to be stored in your garden. A shed will take care of garden tools but unless you're planning on wheeling your bikes and bins in there regularly, you will need to consider where you're going to store them. Make sure to check planning laws and guidelines before building any garden structures, as there are restrictions (see *Resources*).

Enclosure in a garden gives a sense of refuge and privacy.
Architect: Anima | Photographer: Alice Clancy

ELEMENTS OF LANDSCAPE DESIGN

On top of the design principles discussed in previous chapters, there are a number of things you should keep in mind when it comes to landscaping.

THE REGULATING LINE

Lines, either real or imaginary, create the spaces in your landscape. A fence or a hedge makes an obvious border, but the space between two trees or the place where one material meets another can give the sense of a regulating line between two areas. Lines are a powerful design tool as they can be used to create shape and form and can control the movement of the eye and the body around the garden. A well-designed garden, even one that is wild or natural, has defined lines and an underlying order. Straight lines are forceful and lead the eye to a focal point, while curved lines are more informal and relaxed and can add mystery by creating hidden views. Vertical lines are also important as they draw the eye upwards and can make a space feel bigger. Trees and trellises offer the opportunity to do this, while also giving a sense of enclosure.

ENCLOSURE

In order to give people a sense of refuge, a garden must feel enclosed. Enclosures, such as fences, walls, trees and hedges, define the garden and anchor the space. These boundaries do not have to be consistently high around your garden, as the lines you create will identify different areas or zones, which will relate to the enclosures around them. For example, plants and shrubs can enclose a bench, while low fencing or hedging can create a children's play area. Selective planting can also be a great way of screening an obtrusive view or a nosey neighbour.

SIMPLICITY

When it comes to landscaping, less is more. Simplicity brings a sense of calm and restfulness to a garden, whereas a design with too many colours or non-essential features can feel crowded and chaotic. Use the principles of unity and rhythm to ensure clarity and purpose in your design. Pick two or three planting colours and use them throughout your garden. Stick to one or two complimentary colours for walls, fences and hard landscaping. Similarly, choose a few plants that you love and repeat them where suitable. By all means contrast flowers and foliage, but do it as part of an overall plan. Don't forget to think about how each of your plants and their foliage will change with the seasons and plan for the shape and colour of your garden all year round.

When it comes to materials, look to your house for inspiration and continuity. Matching your paving to your floor tiles can give a wonderful indoor/outdoor ambience to both areas. If you have a brick finish on your house, use a similar brick for your garden wall or raised beds.

Try and limit garden features to one area. Build a BBQ or pizza oven close to your seating area or if you have kids' play equipment, keep these bundled together in the same part of the garden.

A WELL-DESIGNED GARDEN, EVEN ONE THAT IS WILD OR NATURAL, HAS DEFINED LINES AND AN UNDERLYING ORDER.

1. The border between paving and lawn provides a regulating line between the two areas. | Architect: DMVF | Photographer: Paul Tierney 2. Trees and plants can provide a great sense of enclosure. | Garden Room: Shomera | Photographer: Gareth Byrne

FINDING YOUR STYLE

Just as with home design, your garden plan starts with you. Your wants and needs, along with the site conditions, are what will determine the shape of your garden. How you develop that shape depends on your own style and on the design of your home, in particular the room that opens onto the garden. If you have a minimalist kitchen with contemporary, clean lines then you may want to continue this style into the garden, whereas a traditional room might lend itself to a more natural or wild garden.

If you have children, then a trampoline or a swing may come top of the list but do consider what you will want from that area once the kids are gone (or maybe, like me, you just plan to have the trampoline to yourself).

INSPIRATION

Spend time in other people's gardens to get an idea of the layout that might work for you and the sort of plants, shrubs and trees you like. Visit parks, botanical gardens and garden centres. Take plenty of photos and if you can't identify plants on your own, show your pictures to horticultural workers in nurseries and garden centres. Plant catalogues are also helpful. And, as always, Houzz, Pinterest, Instagram and gardening blogs are your friends.

PLANTING

When it comes to planting, keep it simple. Instead of trying to cover all available space in one go, wait and see how plants and shrubs grow before filling in the gaps – you can always plant more later. Try to use a good mix of shrubs that flower, fruit and have interesting autumn or winter foliage, along with herbaceous perennials that will come back year after year.

Plant big to small – start with trees, then shrubs and when those are in place, you can add ground plants. Don't be afraid to fill darker spots in your garden – there are plants to suit all variations of light and sunshine. If you have one very shaded side in your garden, plant for those conditions and don't try to match the planting in the other, better-lit parts of your garden.

Plants and shrubs can help soften hard exterior finishes so plant close to your building or use plants in pots and containers to soothe and brighten a rendered or pebble-dashed wall. Creepers and climbers are great for hiding unattractive walls or fences, although a good render or paint job beforehand can go a long way to tidying up a tired boundary.

Don't forget about the birds and the bees. Provide plants that encourage these visitors, such as wisteria, clover, lavender, cat mint and think about building a birdhouse or an insect hotel.

In the end, while it's important to have a plan, there's no substitute for experience – watch your garden grow and let it teach you how to create and curate it. Let your garden evolve with you and every new season will bring new ideas and opportunities.

Materials, such as a set of inexpensive Moroccan tiles, can be used to brighten up a damaged wall.
Photographer: Michael O'Brien

WATCH YOUR GARDEN GROW AND LET IT TEACH YOU HOW TO CREATE AND CURATE IT. LET YOUR GARDEN EVOLVE WITH YOU AND EVERY NEW SEASON WILL BRING NEW IDEAS AND OPPORTUNITIES.

1. Plants and shrubs can help soften walls and other exterior finishes. | Interior Architecture: Maria Fenlon | Photographer: Sean & Yvette
2. Creating an inner garden – the archway invites you in. | Photographer: Michael O'Brien
3. Older houses suit a rambling, overgrown style of garden but this still needs to be planned and cultivated. | Photographer: Philip Lauterbach & Penny Crawford-Collins

SUBURBAN GARDEN

WHO LIVES HERE:
Fiona and her family

LOCATION:
Clontarf, Dublin

PROJECT:
Complete garden redesign

Original garden.

An extensive patio close to the house enables indoor/outdoor living.
All images in case study: Photographer: Ruth Maria Murphy

THE GARDEN

So, back to that pile of muck, now with added grass. It was a fairly standard rectangular suburban garden, complete with unattractive fencing and walls, and a slope that was causing muddy patches where the grass met the existing granite paving. On the other hand, it was a great football pitch, which the kids begged us to leave alone.

We had the following requirements: large shed, in-ground trampoline, built-in BBQ around seating area and a patch of grass big enough to kick a ball around. Although the garden is relatively large, it was a big ask. And that didn't even include my secret plan to fulfil a childhood dream and sneak in a table tennis table. The temptation to ditch the 'less is more' philosophy was strong.

THE DESIGN

The key was to incorporate the visually-obtrusive elements in a zone at the end of the garden where they wouldn't dominate the view from the house. The shed is actually 14 feet deep but because it is only 8 feet wide, it does not command as much attention as I'd feared. And, though it is essentially a shed, the design and colour scheme give it a 'summer room' vibe from a distance.

The end zone also contains the trampoline and a swing seat for capturing the evening sun. At first, I had assumed we would build a terrace at the end of the garden for that same reason but the more we talked about it, the more we realised that it made sense to keep the cooking/eating/lounging area close to the house. As well as aesthetics, this was also for access and convenience as we just didn't see ourselves carrying food and tableware down and back on a regular basis. It was a good call – we now use the BBQ and pizza oven all summer long.

We decided to go big on paving and doubled the size of the existing patio. I recommend this. Work out the paved or decked area you think you'll use and make it bigger. It provides more useable space than lawn and can turn the area into a garden room. When you first see the oversized patio, you might have a little panic attack and think, what have I done, but once you start using it, you'll see what I mean.

The paved area is enclosed with block built and rendered raised beds, which also provide a structure against which we were able to level the remaining lawn. Two granite steps offer a transition from hard to soft landscaping. We still have about half the garden in lawn, which, it turns out, is plenty of space for ball games, especially if you use the trampoline net as a goal.

As far as planting was concerned, we did it all ourselves with very little prior knowledge. We decided on a simple colour scheme of purple and white, went to a local nursery and loaded up on plants, shrubs and trees, keeping in mind what would work in the shady and the sunny sides of the garden. Nothing died so I'm calling that an unparalleled success.

NEW PLAN

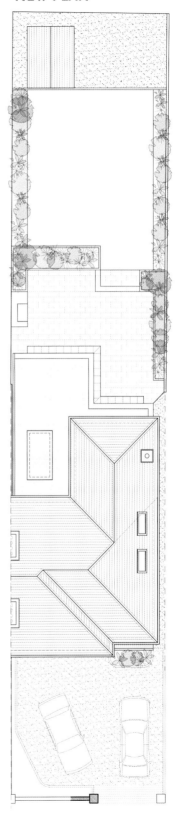

THE COSTS

We didn't spend huge money on the garden. We did it in stages and we did much of the work ourselves and continue to do so. It may not be the most considered or refined design but it's perfect for us and we love it and use it daily. The first thing I do every morning is walk around it, check on the plants and soak up the atmosphere. It's one of the many small daily pleasures our home affords me.

THE FINAL TOUCH

The final touch was the addition of lighting throughout so we can continue to admire the garden all night long. I say 'final' as if there is a single act of completion in the home renovation process. In reality, there may well be a moment where you exhale and put your feet up but your home and garden will continue to evolve and grow with you. And whether you plan it or not, all those skills and tricks you learned along the way will always be on your radar and make demands of you when you least expect it.

In the end, the lighting wasn't the crowning achievement of the garden; I got the table tennis table too!

AND FINALLY

When the urge to change something in your beautiful new home strikes, go with it and experiment – second hand websites are your greatest resource for offloading old furniture as well as finding bargains. Don't be afraid to repaint a room or a wall – it doesn't cost much and it's just a day's work. We recently added a dark grey feature wall to the living area of our extension. It was all over and done within one day and has completely changed the mood of the space.

And the tree in the front garden is a recent addition as well. Now, that storeroom shelving, must get onto that soon …

RESOURCES

This section details links to the government departments, professional bodies and other resources referenced throughout the book. You can also find more information on **www.makethehomeyoulove.com**.

ARCHITECTURE

Open House Festival
www.openhouseworldwide.org

RIAI Simon Open Door initiative
www.simonopendoor.ie

Royal Institute of the Architects of Ireland (RIAI)
www.riai.ie

Royal Society of Ulster Architects (RSUA)
www.rsua.org.uk

RSUA and PLACE Ask an Architect Week
www.askanarchitect-ni.com

Royal Institute of British Architects' bookshop
www.ribabookshops.com

BUILDING CONTROL

Republic of Ireland
www.housing.gov.ie

Building Control Management System (BCMS)
www.localgov.ie

Northern Ireland
www.buildingcontrol-ni.com

CONSERVATION

Irish Georgian Society
www.igs.ie

National Inventory of Architectural Heritage
www.buildingsofireland.ie

Historical Properties Advice Series
www.chg.gov.ie/heritage/built-heritage/architectural-heritage-advisory-service/advice-for-owners

For listed buildings in Northern Ireland, check local authorities
www.planningni.gov.uk

CONTRACTS

Royal Institute of the Architects of Ireland
www.riai.ie

Northern Ireland: Joint Contracts Tribunal
www.jctltd.co.uk

COSTS

Construction and renovation costs in the Republic of Ireland
www.riai.ie

Society of Chartered Surveyors Ireland
www.scsi.ie

Royal Institute of Chartered Surveyors
www.rics.org

VAT rates and tax incentives in the Republic of Ireland
www.revenue.ie

VAT rates in Northern Ireland
www.gov.uk

Declan Doyle, Quantity Surveyor
www.oconnordoyle.com

DESIGN

Houzz
www.houzz.ie

Instagram
www.instagram.com

Pinterest
www.pinterest.com

Selfbuild Ireland
www.selfbuild.ie

Melanie Flood, Eco Interiors, Kitchen Designer
www.ecointeriors.ie

ENERGY EFFICIENCY

Sun position calculator
www.suncalc.org

Passive House Association of Ireland
www.phai.ie

Sustainable Energy Authority of Ireland
www.seai.ie

GRANTS

Sustainable Energy Authority of Ireland
www.seai.ie

Northern Ireland Housing Executive
www.nihe.gov.uk

Revenue Commissioners
www.revenue.ie

HM Revenue and Customs
www.gov.uk

Local Area Planning Office
www.planningni.gov.uk

Irish Georgian Society
www.igs.ie

HEALTH AND SAFETY

Health and Safety Authority
www.hsa.ie

Health and Safety Executive of Northern Ireland
www.hseni.gov.uk

PLANNING

An Bord Pleanála
www.pleanala.ie

Department of Housing, Planning, Community
and Local Government
www.housing.gov.ie

Local Area Planning Office
www.planningni.gov.uk

Planning Appeals Commission
www.pacni.gov.uk

ACKNOWLEDGEMENTS

This book has been a collaborative process between many talented and dedicated professionals. First and foremost, I would like to thank Colm, Lisa and John for their help and guidance and for being such brilliant architects in the first place. Also, the whole team at DMVF for fitting my endless requests into their busy schedules.

Thanks to everyone at The O'Brien Press, who made the whole process easy, smooth and, most of all, fun. To Michael and Ivan O'Brien for believing in the book from the start, and to Aoife Walsh for putting it all together.

Thanks to my patient and thorough editor, Aoife Barrett, for getting it right and for all those late nights (see, I told you I'd thank you for those one day).

Thanks to Tanya Ross for designing such a beautiful book.

Thanks to photographer, Ruth Maria Murphy, for making my house and so many others look so magical.

Thanks to Eadaoin Patton, Dominic Morris, the RIAI and the RSUA for advice and proof-reading.

Thanks to all the architects featured – John Feely, Amanda Bone, ALW, Plus Architecture, Patti O'Neill, Broadstone, David Flynn, McNally Morris Architects, Anima, Alan Bennett Architects, John McLaughlin, Optimise Design and Bright Designs.

Thanks to all the homeowners who gave us a glimpse into their lives, in particular those featured in the case studies – Sarah Clarke, Naomi Morley, Nico Dowling, Anne Flood, Imelda Murphy, Patti O'Neill and Peter O'Reilly.

Thanks to photographers, Gareth Byrne, Paul Tierney, Ros Kavanagh, Sarah Fyffe, Infinity Media, Laura O'Gorman, Derek Robinson, Aisling McCoy, Alice Clancy, Aidan Monaghan, Sean & Yvette, Barbara Corsico, Peter O'Reilly, Philip Lauterbach, Penny Crawford-Collins, Bradley Quinn, Donal Murphy, Alan Bennett, Dominic Morris and Kevin Woods.

Thanks to designers, Maria Fenlon, Maven, Suzie McAdam, Kingston Lafferty Design, Veronica Clarke, Little Design House, On the Square Emporium, Dust Design, Newcastle Design, Melanie Flood of Eco Interiors, KHS Landscaping, Shalford Interiors and Shomera. Thanks also to stylists, Marlene Wessels and Ciara O'Halloran, and quantity surveyor, Declan Doyle.

Thanks to Amanda Kavanagh for the photos featured on pages 36, 43 (bottom photo), 48 (bottom photo), 127 and 151, all of which first appeared in *Image Interiors & Living* magazine.

And last, but by no means least, thanks to John, James, Anna and Harry, without whom there would be no home in the first place.